TRUTH
FOR
ALL
TIME

CW01090889

ON BEING
A PASTOR

A THEOLOGY OF SHEPHERDING

IAN S. McNAUGHTON

DayOne

© 2023 Ian S. McNaughton

ISBN 978-1-84625-752-0

All Scripture quotations, unless stated otherwise, are from The Holy Bible,
New King James Version Copyright © 1982 by Thomas Nelson, Inc.
Used by Permission. All rights reserved.

British Library Cataloguing in Publication Data available

Published by Day One Publications
Telephone 01568 613 740
Toll Free 888 329 6630 (North America)
email—sales@dayone.co.uk
web site—www.dayone.co.uk

All rights reserved
No part of this publication may be reproduced, or stored in a retrieval system, or
transmitted, in any form or by any means, mechanical, electronic, photocopying,
recording or otherwise, without the prior permission of Day One Publications.

Printed by 4edge Limited

Dedicated to

*the churches in which I learned the craft of a Pastor
and those where I preached in retirement allowing me
to hone my skills and to research the Scriptures
for God's wisdom and Christ's gospel aided by the Holy Spirit,
as an under-shepherd of Christ's people;*

and

Violet my dear wife

*and to all God's under-shepherds in Christ who,
as fellow pilgrims in the journey of faith, hope and love,
experience goodness and mercy all the days of their life (Psalm 23).*

'For I say, through the grace given to me, to everyone who is among you, not to think of himself more highly than he ought to think, but to think soberly, as God has dealt to each one a measure of faith … Having then gifts differing according to the grace that is given to us, let us use them: if prophecy, let us prophesy in proportion to our faith; or ministry, let us use it in our ministering; he who teaches, in teaching; he who exhorts, in exhortation; he who gives, with liberality; he who leads, with diligence; he who shows mercy, with cheerfulness … Be kindly affectionate to one another with brotherly love, in honour giving preference to one another; not lagging in diligence, fervent in spirit, serving the Lord; rejoicing in hope, patient in tribulation, continuing steadfastly in prayer; distributing to the needs of the saints, given to hospitality. Bless those who persecute you; bless and do not curse. Rejoice with those who rejoice, and weep with those who weep. Be of the same mind toward one another. Do not set your mind on high things, but associate with the humble. Do not be wise in your own opinion.'

(Romans 12)

In this wonderful book the Rev. McNaughton is at his best as he draws upon over forty years of pastoral and ministerial experience. Although written with the aim of 'helping the novice and young to prepare for pastoral ministry', it would be a mistake to think this is a book exclusively for that group. This material deserves (and should have) the widest possible readership. This book will, as the author says in his foreword, help 'elders, deacons and church members to understand the work and trials of a full-time calling'. Though the chapters are short, a lot is packed into each one as every possible base is covered. There are several very helpful appendices which expand on the material presented, giving food for thought. Chapter 11 on public worship should be printed separately in tract form and sent to every church and University Christian Union in the land! It is with great pleasure I wholeheartedly commend this very up-to-date and relevant book. It reads well and will reward the reader immensely.

Pastor Billy McCurrie
Aughton Park Baptist Church, Ormskirk

There are many books and articles about the pastorate, of variable quality, and, in some cases, questionable value. But Ian McNaughton's book is one that is not only valuable, it is challenging, inspiring and practically helpful for anyone who is considering entering the pastoral ministry. He writes from many years of experience, but also with a firm dependence on biblical principles. He emphasises the importance of calling and that pastors are sent from God. Both of these matters are vitally necessary, although, sadly, they are much debated in some circles today. His emphasis on the work of the Holy Spirit and the fact that we are in a spiritual warfare are also necessary correctives in these far too individualistic self-help days. His first appendix, 'Ten reasons *not* to be a pastor', is another helpful challenge to any who may think that the pastorate is an easy option. As one who has spent much of his life in the pastorate I wish that this book had been available when I started and I commend it warmly.

Rev. Dr Ian M Densham

It is essential that all pastors have a heart for their congregation. What is rarer is to find a man with a heart for pastors such as Ian McNaughton displays in this book. He writes from experience and conviction as he seeks to help them in their theology and practice and personal life with God. There is much here in a small compass. All new and aspiring pastors should study the matter in this book. Regarding the content: it is very good!

John Palmer, Pastor emeritus
Bethany Evangelical Church, Leigh, Lancs.

Ian McNaughton's work is very challenging to those of us called to pastoral ministry: the vital importance of our own personal walk with the Lord is a constant underlying implication, which is brought out into the open at several key places in the book. At the same time, we are reminded of the immense privilege that is ours to have such a calling, even though at times the position can certainly be a lonely one. Ian refuses to duck potentially contentious issues, and offers wise guidance on making unavoidable decisions. I found especially thought-provoking, amongst many other things, his comments on the current debate about conversion therapy. The final chapter is a necessary call to the whole church to pray for their pastors: the humility which recognises this dire need is to be commended.

Dr Jonathan Bayes
Pastor Stanton Lees Chapel, Derbyshire

Contents

Prologue

'Preachers are born not made. This is an absolute. You will
never teach a man to be a preacher if he is not already one.'
(D. Martyn Lloyd-Jones)

'The ministerial work must be carried on for God and the
salvation of souls, not for any private ends of our own.'
(Richard Baxter)[1]

*'I say, through the grace given to me, to everyone who is among you, not to
think of himself more highly than he ought to think, but to think soberly,
as God has dealt to each one a measure of faith.'* (Romans 12:3)

The high calling of pastors and evangelical preachers is grasped
in Luther's quote; 'If I could today become a king or emperor, I
would not give up my office as a preacher.'[2] He had a high view
of preaching and would have felt as Paul who said, 'For Christ did not
send me to baptise, but to preach the gospel,' and again, 'Necessity is laid
upon me; yes, woe is me if I do not preach the gospel!' (1 Corinthians 1:17;
9:16). That the power of the Holy Spirit was in Luther's life was seen in the
zeal he had for preaching. 'Frequently he preached several times a week,
often two or more times a day. For example he preached 117 sermons in
Wittenberg in 1522 and 137 sermons the next year. In 1528 he preached
almost 200 times, and from 1529 we have 212 sermons. So the average

---

1   Richard Baxter, *The Reformed Pastor* (Edinburgh: The Banner of Truth Trust, 1979), p. 111.
2   J. Piper, *The Legacy of Sovereign Joy* (IVP, 2000), p. 86.

in those four years was one sermon every two and half days.'[3] Contrast that with the average pastor today. He might preach a total of 100 a year (but that is unlikely). Luther elevated the biblical text itself far above the teachings of commentators and church fathers. This idea, that the Bible could be understood by all Christian believers and that they have a right to interpret it, brought Lutheranism, Anglicanism and the other Protestant churches into being.[4] Today's Protestants must not go it alone, as it were. Rather they must consult the Reformed Confessions such as the Westminster Confession of Faith 1645, the Savoy Declaration of Faith and Order 1658, and the London Baptist Confession of 1689, with their catechisms. All exhibit a mature Protestant and Evangelical theology and practice. The Continental Protestant confessions of faith are also of great value: The Three Forms of Unity, The Belgic Confession, The Canons of Dort, and The Heidelberg Catechism, and are accepted as official statements of doctrine by many of the Reformed churches. Luther's legacy was to free us from the superstition and errors that Roman Catholicism had built. He preached justification by faith only from Romans chapter 1 and discovered it first in his study of Book of Psalms.[5]

I write this book after (over) forty-five years of preaching and pastoring evangelical churches in the UK. I write to help the novice and the young to prepare for lifelong ministry in local churches. I trust that it may also help elders, deacons and church members to understand the work and trials of a full-time calling. The Christian pastor is tasked to teach, help, support, protect, and to care for the local church as Christ's under-shepherd while depending always on the Spirit of God daily (cf. Galatians 5:16–26). The equipping of the saints for the work of ministry has a means to an end, viz. the edifying of the body of Christ in order to achieve a unity that is of God, i.e. the growth of the church both spiritually and doctrinally.

---

3 Ibid, p. 87.
4 Alister McGrath, *Christianity's Dangerous Idea* (New York: Harper, 2007).
5 Especially Psalms 32 and 130. These and others Luther called 'the Pauline Psalms'.

That is paramount. When it comes to church life the pastor has his own special place and function. The position of each part of the redeemed body is not self-determined but placed there by Christ Himself as head of the churches. The mature believer acknowledges and accepts this. The pastor must do his part and fulfil that function. Church growth has three parts to it: (1) *'till we all come to the unity of the faith'*, which is the appropriation of God's love and the looking to Christ only for grace and salvation; (2) *'to the knowledge of the Son of God'*, which is the apprehension of Christs glory, viz. His eternal Sonship, priesthood and kingship; (3) *'to a perfect man'*, which is ours by grace alone through faith alone, 'eagerly waiting for the adoption, the redemption of our body' while our ascended Saviour, at the right hand of the majesty on high, is interceding until the great day of full transformation is reached (Romans 8:23; Hebrews 7:25; 12:1b–2a). What is the church? It is *universal in its extent*, not buildings or societies or institutions; rather, it includes people from every continent, nation, culture. Nor is it limited to the West, but citizens of East and West, North and South are within and it embraces all people groups and tribes. It is also *local in its expression:* Paul writes to Philippi, i.e. to a local church with local leaders thus, because neighbourhood churches are located around the world made up of people who live and work locally. It is *personal in experience:* the true church is made up of converts who being born again are justified by faith and adopted into God's family knowing Jesus Christ as their personal Saviour.

The late Rev. William Still of Aberdeen said: 'The pastor feeds the flock upon God's Word; the bulk of pastoral work is therefore through the ministry of the Word. Only the residue of the problems and difficulties remaining require to be dealt with thereafter. His primary task is to *feed* the flock in green pastures (Psalm 23). This will take all his intellectual, mental, spiritual and emotional powers to *care* for the flock who are ill and seek the flock when astray. The ultimate aim (of all pastoral work) is to lead God's people to offer themselves up to Him in total devotion of worship and service. All that many spiritually sick people need is a good balanced diet and a disciplined routine; expository preaching solves all problems in time' (p. 36). 'The most fruitful pastoral duty is to help people (of all sorts) to live together: all are of equal value to God' (p. 40). 'Some people are beyond you—not God of course. Rather there are limits to your abilities and calling.' Remember 'some only want the fruit of Christianity not its roots—cut flowers only!' The goal of preaching 'is a means to an end, which is not merely that we should be right and clean (justified and forgiven) but that we may be His, which involves personal relationship in love. God wants us for Himself and to that end He brings us to birth in Christ' (p. 51). 'A true Christian fellowship is a place where stray cats and dogs find a home. It is a hospital, where the only sin is to hide your wounds from the doctor and the nurse. The true pastor's job is to strip all the fearful ones however gently, faithfully, and all the hypocritical ones of their camouflage and cloaks' (p. 46). 'Remember the pastor is not a spiritual doctor. The tension in his work is between the ministry of the Word and the care of the soul. The Holy Spirit is the Doctor. The work is done through a dead man ministering the living word in the power of the Spirit, wooed into the midst by the prayers of the saints. The soul is never so much in private with God as when sitting in church being sifted, searched, corrected, fed by the ministry of the word' (p. 49).[6]

Pastors are to speak as the oracles of God and act as under-shepherds to the flock, and those who preach the Word of God to others are to feed them God's truth and divine will:

If anyone speaks, let him speak as the oracles of God. If anyone ministers, let him do it as with the ability which God supplies, that in all things God may be glorified through Jesus Christ, to whom belong the glory and the dominion forever and ever. Amen. (1 Peter 4:11)

---

6 William Still, *The Work of the Pastor*, preface (Fearn: Christian Focus, 2001), pages as marked.

The word *oracle* is used in several ways in the Bible. The Hebrew word translated oracle means a parable or proverb. In 2 Samuel 16:23 the word oracle is a translation of a Hebrew word that means 'word' or 'utterance'. It refers to a communication from God given for guidance. A different Hebrew word is translated *oracle* in Jeremiah 23:33–38 (*burden*, KJV). This word means a thing lifted up; it can refer to a prophetic utterance as well as a physical burden. Jeremiah uses this double meaning and speaks of the prophetic oracle as a burden that is difficult to bear. When the New Testament speaks of oracles, it sometimes refers to the Old Testament or some portion of it (Acts 7:38; Romans 3:2). Hebrews 5:12 uses the term to speak of both the Old Testament revelation and the Word made flesh, Jesus Christ. 1 Peter 4:11 warns that the teacher of Christian truths must speak as an oracle of God because he has a message from God and not his own opinions.

In Ezekiel 24 the prophet was called by God to be a sign to the exiles of Judah; he was warned that his wife, *the desire of his eyes*, would die. She died on the evening of that day, and, contrary to all normal reactions, he was commanded not to mourn. This was surely a very hard command to obey. When the people asked the meaning of his strange behaviour, he told them that their sons and daughters would be killed, and they were not to mourn (v. 23). What Ezekiel was commanded illustrates the degree of personal sacrifice and separation from ordinary life that the ministers of God are often required to endure as one called to preach. Ezekiel obeyed as commanded (v. 18b):

Ezekiel is a sign to you; according to all that he has done you shall do; and when this comes, you shall know that I am the Lord GOD. (v. 24)

An *oracle* is a person with a biblical message uttered in the Spirit. Preaching is more than a brother just giving a 'word', because it is not enough for a man simply to preach from the Bible. He should also have the assurance that he is presenting the particular message intended by God for that audience at that time. A man who is called to preach must be sure that the words he speaks are the very words God would have him say—a messenger as Haggai the prophet of old with the Lord's message to the Lord's people. He is one who has received a gift and is a custodian called to speak in the best interest of the One who chose him. Anyone who performs any kind of service to God should do it with the humble recognition that it is God who empowers. We have nothing which we did not receive. All service should be performed so that God gets the credit (Psalm 115:1).

No pastor is perfect nor does any have all the gifts for a flawless career; all 'come short of the glory of God'. However, there is a calling and there is a gift of ministry given to the local churches by Christ Jesus for their edification, protection, preservation and proclamation of gospel truth. The high and holy calling to preach and to pastor Christ's sheep as an under-shepherd is not easy but it comes with the necessary grace and strength when faith, love and hope are present. The daily need to take up our cross and follow Jesus is a life's calling without which our service is lacking in holiness and the Spirit's presence.

Do not I love Thee, dearest Lord?
  Behold my heart and see;
And cast each hated idol down,
  That dares to rival Thee.

Do not I love Thee, O my soul?
  Then let me nothing love;
Dead be my heart to every joy
  When Jesus cannot move.

Is not Thy name melodious still
  To my attentive ear?
Do I not in Thy word delight
  The Saviour's voice to hear?

Hast Thou a lamb in all Thy flock,
  I would disdain to feed?
Hast Thou a foe, before whose face
  I'd fear Thy cause to plead?

Thou know'st I love Thee, dearest Lord,
  But Oh, I long to soar
Far from the sphere of mortal joys,
  And learn to love Thee more!

(Philip Doddridge, 1702–1751)

Pastors are to visit the sick and wash their feet: love them and they will love you. Preach and 'speak as the oracle of God' with humility and grace evident by love and compassion toward the listeners:

The elders who are among you I exhort, I who am a fellow elder and a witness of the sufferings of Christ, and also a partaker of the glory that will be revealed: Shepherd the flock of God which is among you, serving as overseers, not by compulsion but willingly, not for dishonest gain but eagerly; nor as being lords over those entrusted to you, but being examples to the flock; and when the Chief Shepherd appears, you will receive the crown of glory that does not fade away (1 Peter 5:1–4).

The pastor's message is about salvation. Christ is not only 'mighty to save' those who repent, but He is able to bring us to repentance. He will carry those to heaven who believe. Thus it is essential that pastors preach the word in season and out of season, for:

How then shall they call on Him in whom they have not believed? And how shall they believe in Him of whom they have not heard? And how shall they hear without a preacher? And how shall they preach unless they are sent? As it is written: *'How beautiful are the feet of those who preach the gospel of peace, Who bring glad tidings of good things!'* (Romans 10:14–15)

This book stresses the urgent need for full-time pastors, who are called, committed and willing, as Christ leads, to serve their local church at whatever cost. Part-time ministries are unable to 'be watchful in all things' as other responsibilities take up their time and energy. Fulfilling a full-time ministry demands courage as well as faith; strength as well as will; anointing as well as education; calling as well as the new birth; time as well as ambition.

THANKS

I am grateful for the help received from Mr Peter Stafford (friend and freelance editor) and to those pastors whose peer reviews (see the front of this book) of this manuscript have been of great encouragement in days of trial. And not least, thanks go to Dr Ian Densham and Dr Robert Beckett whose support has been invaluable in preparing this manuscript for the printer.

1. A fearful task

'Sound judgement and solid experience must instruct you: gentle manners and loving affections must sway you; firmness and courage must be manifest; and tenderness and sympathy must not be lacking.' (C.H. Spurgeon)[7]

'God have mercy upon all of us who are called to preach if we fail in the exercise of this ministry.' (D. Martyn Lloyd-Jones, *Christian Unity*, p. 207)[8]

'I have always been amazed at the readiness of certain young ministers to advise their brethren on preaching and pastoral matters, "Who is sufficient for these things?"' (D. Martyn Lloyd-Jones)[9]

'He who rules over men must be just, ruling in the fear of God.' (2 Samuel 23:3b)

'Fulfil your ministry.' (2 Timothy 4:2–5)

Preaching is a timeless link between God and man, and is the medium through which God speaks to His people. A prophetic word from God is the Lord's message through Lord's messenger (Haggai 1:13). He is not so much a man speaking *about* God as *for* Him. Through preaching God is using human lips to speak and is the divinely

---

7   C.H. Spurgeon, *Lectures to My Students* (Edinburgh: Marshall, Morgan & Scott, 1958), p. 32.

8   Sargent, *'Gems from Martyn Lloyd-Jones'*, p. 244.

9   D.M. Lloyd-Jones, *Preaching and Preachers* (London: Hodder & Stoughton, 1976), preface.

appointed means of spiritual blessings when accompanied by the Holy Spirit. There is a low view of preaching that regards it as merely a man talking and giving some opinions and comments, even displaying personal prejudice. However, the Bible views it as utterances sent by God: 'How shall they hear without a preacher? And how shall they preach except they are sent?' (Romans 10:14b–15).

Preaching is a high and fearful task. For it is not about human opinions or ideas but a faithful reporting of God's mind as revealed in the Holy Bible. It is a divine calling. It is the 'sacrament of the Word' and the pulpit is 'the throne of the word of God'. The Reformers never set preaching and worship in opposition. They put the sermon where the mass had been and the pulpit where the altar had been. Without the priority of preaching, worship services can degenerate into a liturgical routine. Some place the Eucharist or the mass as the focal point of Christian worship with no need for hearing the Word of God; this the Protestant Reformers rejected and so must evangelicals.

Preaching speaks for God

Preaching is God's chief way of announcing His will to us: 'And as you go, preach, saying "The kingdom of heaven is at hand"' (Matthew 10:7). The preacher is the Lord's herald, so the authority of the preacher is not in himself for he is a bearer of news from God (Greek *kērux*, a herald and *kērussō*, 'I proclaim' or 'I preach'). In the old world the herald was of considerable importance. He was the king's envoy through whom he made his will and laws known. The preacher is God's messenger and by means of him God can reveal Himself in the 'here and now' through His inspired Word. John the Baptist was a herald and he spoke of the One who came down from heaven and not for himself. It is the pastor's calling to shine light and truth on Jesus Christ the Saviour of the world. John the Baptist insisted that Jesus Christ had to increase and that he (John) had to decrease (John 3:30): 'John's ministry laboured ceaselessly to point men and women to the Lord, and to make them realise His true worth. In doing this, John realised that he must keep himself in the background. For John (a servant of Christ) to seek to attract attention to himself is really a form of disloyalty.'[10]

Preaching proclaims the knowledge of God

The preacher's task is to teach what the Bible text says and to explain it in the light of the whole counsel of God so that it is understood. Preaching is meant to feed the flock of God. It is not as a series of short stories about one's private life loosely joined together by some text or other but rather a discourse that feeds the soul with the meat and milk of the Word. It is like the sacred manna on which Israel fed in the wilderness, not as 'cheese and biscuits' but as a main meal! It is not a 'PS' (postscript) but the main banquet where God who is the Almighty and the Eternal One—our Father in heaven—is made known. His mercy as well as His love is proclaimed and He is offered to sinners in the gospel of His Son Jesus Christ on repentance and faith. Preaching is to be directed to the mind, conveying truth; directed to the conscience, for here the conviction of sin lies and here the peace of God and forgiveness of sins is felt. It is more than education or natural insight and has to do with the salvation of souls when the Word of God is preached (1 Peter 1:23). When we preach what God is, as well as who He is the conscience is stirred and repentance is recognised as important unto salvation. Preaching is more than a few thoughts that occur to me through the week! Nor is it a little advice. It is, as Bernard Lord Manning put it, 'a manifestation of the Incarnate Word from the written Word by the spoken word.'[11]

---

10 Nelson, CD_ROM: The Holy Bible, New King James Version, copyright 1982 by Thomas Nelson, Inc. It should be noted that John is the last and greatest of the Old Testament prophets and now that the Christ has been revealed he moves back as his ministry is ending under the new covenant dispensation with Christ Jesus as our Prophet, Priest and King.

11 Bernard Lord Manning (source unavailable) see https://books.google.co.uk/books?id =AzJTAwAAQBAJ & pg=PT27&lpg=PT27&dq=Bernard+Lord+Manning+put+it

Preaching declares the salvation of God

Preaching differs from a lecture for its aim is not simply to inform but to convey the truths of Scripture and to 'humble the sinner, exalt the Saviour and to promote holiness'.[12] Nor is it to be treated in the same way as a lecture or an after-dinner speech. A lecture will inform the mind, but a sermon goes beyond this as it aims to motivate the will and is intended to motivate the hearer to come to the Saviour in repentance and faith. It calls for a believing response to the free offer of the gospel. This free offer of the gospel is to sound forth from the lips of Christ's heralds and the listeners are to be exhorted to 'be doers of the word and not hearers only, deceiving yourselves' (James 1:22). God expects us to respond well (i.e. in faith and repentance) to what He says through faithful preaching (Acts 17:30). The believing response will save his soul and will glorify God when the greatness of His lordship over us and the beauty of His love for us are recognised. The proclamation of God the Almighty and His Son's death and resurrection are to be the preacher's constant industry:

Preach the word! Be ready in season and out of season. Convince, rebuke, exhort, with all longsuffering and teaching. For the time will come when they will not endure sound doctrine, but according to their own desires, because they have itching ears, they will heap up for themselves teachers; and they will turn their ears away from the truth, and be turned aside to fables. (2 Timothy 4:2–4)

Preaching calls for a response

Preaching and worship belong together because through these channels people grow in the knowledge of God, and are encouraged to praise

---

12 Charles Simeon was a renowned preacher for 54 years at Holy Trinity Church Cambridge, until his death in 1836. In 1832 he published 21 volumes of sermon 'skeletons' or outlines, with some 2,536 sermon outlines. This work was called 'Horae Homileticae'. Simeon had three stated objectives in his preaching: 'to humble the sinner, to exalt the Saviour and to promote holiness.' https //books.google.co.uk/books/about/Selections_from_the_Sermons_of_Charles_S

their Maker and obey His will. Hearers cannot be neutral before God's Word. To detach ourselves or switch off will only harm. It is in God's house, where God's Word is heard, that souls are saved, and as Jonathan Edwards says, 'Let us be thankful for the Sabbath because God has given it to us for the care of our souls.' This is a day when God 'especially confers His grace and blessing' and this blessing is for those who 'consciously sanctify it. God blessed the sixth day of creation; how much more will He bless the first of Christ's resurrection and delight to honour it? When the Sabbath is well kept, there the cause of true religion will flourish.'[13] We are to come under the Word, not to criticise or to sleep but to 'draw near to hear' so as to be blessed for time and eternity (Ecclesiastes 5:1). A right attitude is important. If we come to worship in order to glorify God through praise and to humble ourselves before Him in prayer, then surely we will look forward with a true heart to hearing His Word preached and expounded? Our response will glorify God if we recognise the greatness of His lordship over us and the beauty of His love for us: 'The sacrifices of God are a broken spirit, a broken and a contrite heart—these O God, You will not despise' (Psalm 51:17). We cannot be neutral before God's Word nor are we are to apply what is heard to our neighbour but we are to accept it for ourselves. Hearing the gospel Good News we are to believe it for justification. God will not believe it for us!

The need to trust God always

Serving Jesus Christ means that we are to trust God at all times and there is need to trust our Saviour Jesus Christ when disillusionment is known, or weariness is setting in, or we are tempted to lose heart, or injured by friends … the list could go on. At such times, the psalmist has good advice for us: trust the Lord God at all times.

Psalm 125 is one of the 15 'Songs of Ascent' in Book 5 of the Psalms. It reflects the historically difficult times Israel faced as it persevered in

---

13 Jonathan Edwards, *Works*, Vol. 2 (Edinburgh: The Banner of Truth Trust, 1974), pp. 101–102.

the faith of its fathers and in the conflicts with the surrounding heathen nations and enemies of Jehovah God. The whole psalm is an expression of strong confidence in God's divine protection which evokes trust in times of trouble. Trust in God brings confidence and secures peace for us. Thus the psalm could be entitled 'Peace from divine help'. However, trusting in the Lord does not come naturally to us; trusting, said Martin Luther, 'is the plain way to God'. It begins at conversion and it is necessary in the walk of faith, the way of faith and the work of faith (James 2:26). God says to us, 'Trust Me at all times.' If we are to trust God it is necessary to depend on Him, to remain confident, patient and hopeful.

1. BE DEPENDENT

Self-sufficiency is a sin of pride and some think they need to trust in no one but themselves as they look to their own resources. Some trust money. Others depend on intellect. Yet others rely on family. However, those who trust in Christ depend on Him for protection (Psalm 125:2); strength (v.3; cf. 2 Corinthians 3:5); encouragement (v.4; cf. 2 Corinthians 4:16–18) and inner peace (v.5b). In the Christian life we are dependent on Christ and His Spirit for help in our 'spiritual battle' (Ephesians 6:10–20). Christians are sure Christ will supply all their needs (Philippians 4:19) and will keep them strong in the faith (1 Peter 1:5). The Christian life is one of total dependence on our Saviour. Prayer is of vital importance here (v.4). However, it must also be *normal*. Thus we should pray daily and pray 'without ceasing' (Psalm 62:8; Ephesians 6:18). We cannot keep ourselves secure, but the Bible makes it clear that 'our sufficiency is from God' (2 Corinthians 3:5). We must be dependent on Him for everything that is required to finish the race set before us (Hebrews 12:1–2).

2. BE CONFIDENT

Confidence in Christ Himself is essential if trusting is to bear good fruit. Are we confident that our Saviour is able to keep us from falling? If so, what does that require on our part? Remember, trusting in someone entails the conviction that they can be fully depended upon, so their character and their motives are of vital importance. We must take into account the integrity of God's character and Christ's ability to give the help we require. These vital qualities are found in Jesus Christ our Saviour (Ephesians 3:20; Philippians 1:6). Exercising faith will place our future in Christ's hands. It has been said that 'Christ Jesus is our Trustee and He has promised to manage all our affairs and to manage them well'.[14] Thus if we deal with God it must be on the basis of a confidence that holds fast to the Rock of Ages. All God's heralds face many trials and there are times when they do not know what to do or where to turn. This is then another opportunity to fully depend on our Saviour's love for us and His promises to us (Proverbs 3:5–6; Psalm 32:10; Matthew 6:5–15; 2 Corinthians 5:7). Christians must place their full and unreserved confidence in Christ.

3. BE PATIENT

Trust without patience is putting 'self' on the throne; however, exercising patience is allowing Christ to sit on the throne of our hearts. If we really trust Christ we will triumph over our impatience. There is need for us to be longsuffering so it may do its perfect work (James 1:4; cf. Psalm 123:1–2). Patience is not procrastination (delaying) but faith in operation (Hebrews 10:36; 11:13–16). It is good to remember that God can answer our prayers in three ways: *yes*, *no*, or *wait!* (1 John 3:22; 5:14). Patience is the fruit of the Holy Spirit and is a friend to self-control (Galatians 5:22,23), it rejoices in hope, is patient in tribulation and continues steadfastly in prayer (Romans 12:12). Thus Christians must place their full and unreserved trust in Christ their Saviour. We must be dependent on Him for everything required to finish the race (Hebrews 12:1–2). The Christian is called to exercise the grace of patience while awaiting the call to come home to heaven. Matthew Henry said, 'All

---

14 Unknown.

that deal with God must deal upon trust, and He will give comfort to those only that give credit to Him.'

4. BE HOPEFUL

Hope is of vital importance to all who would walk in faith and trust because hope is faith plus patience. Without it there is a temptation to doubt and anxiety is present in the soul. 'Hope is 'set before us' in the gospel to facilitate trust, 'as an anchor of the soul, both sure and steadfast' (Hebrews 6:19). It is always about tomorrow (Romans 8:24) and the object of hope is God Himself, and thus trust in the 'God of hope' is to be renewed and revived day by day, for 'He remains faithful' (2 Timothy 2:13; cf. Psalm 62:8; 138:8). John Bunyan said, 'Hope is never ill when faith is well.'

Now may the God of peace who brought up our Lord Jesus from the dead, that great Shepherd of the sheep, through the blood of the everlasting covenant, make you complete in every good work to do His will, working in you what is well pleasing in His sight, through Jesus Christ, to whom be glory forever and ever. Amen. (Hebrews 13:20–21)

2. A calling

'…it is most dangerous for a man to be a lay preacher.'
(D. Martyn Lloyd-Jones, *Saving Faith*, p. 289) [15]

'If you would find the men who serve God the best, you must look for the men of the most faith.' (C. H. Spurgeon) [16]

'If you want joy be an itinerant preacher. If you want heartache be a leader of an assembly!' (J. N. Darby)

'For you see your calling, brethren, that not many wise according to the flesh, not many mighty, not many noble, are called. But God has chosen the foolish things of the world to put to shame the wise, and God has chosen the weak things of the world to put to shame the things which are mighty; and the base things of the world and the things which are despised God has chosen, and the things which are not, to bring to nothing the things that are, that no flesh should glory in His presence.' (1 Corinthians 1:26–29)

A pastor's call is the main issue for men in the ministry and it is good to grasp that in this vocation as in other professions there are 'horses for courses'. Charles Spurgeon wanted pastors to be hard-working and all-round theologians with a shepherd's heart. This is still required today.

Calling and assurance are what keeps men where God wants them. The demands of a full workload, stresses and pastoral concerns

---

15 Sargent, *Gems from Martyn Lloyd-Jones*, p. 232.
16 *Morning & Evening*, March 7.

are all constant issues and the lack of days off along with oversight responsibilities contribute to a very busy life. Sabbaticals are good for conscientious and diligent men. Weariness and disappointments are added factors and can contribute to a loss of zeal and commitment. The hidden factor is satanic attacks. This is off the radar for the majority of ordinary members and especially for the non-members who do not grasp this spiritual element fully. I knew a good man who had been a Sunday School teacher, deacon and elder, all in the same local church, but it was not until he took on the full-time pastorate (in the same church) that he said, 'I did not know how difficult and demanding it was'—or something in that vein! Calvin saw this difficulty in practice when he reassigned his evangelists who found the work too onerous, and made them school teachers. The minister's calling and our independent church polity should be biblically based. Part-time men are acceptable if called as church planters as tent-makers or as evangelists, but the pastoral ministry demands full-time labour with the support of a committed (saved) and supportive wife.

Those who have oversight in our local churches as pastors/teachers are to be gifted and called (Ephesians 4:1–3). There will be an *internal call* and an *external call* and both are necessary. I have known men who feel the first but do not pass the second test. Others are intellectually gifted and studious in nature but have no assurance of the Spirit's leading. The *internal call* is an anchor which will hold fast when the storms rage, while an *external call* is the recognition given by the local church and its eldership that the necessary graces and gifts for a leadership role have been (at least in seed form) seen in the prospective pastor. This latter call will also help a pastor's resolve to keep to his calling when opposition raises its head against him. It must be added here that prospective men are to be seen as gracious, self-sacrificing and having a willingness to work and study without constant oversight. Pastors are chosen and commissioned by God in Christ Jesus and as stewards they must not seek office for power! Personal agendas and plans are not welcomed in the churches of Christ (see Appendix 1, below).[17]

This honour is not to be self-appointed but God-given; not self-chosen but God-called: 'No man takes this honour to himself, but he who is called by God' (Hebrews 5:4).

The pastoral office

Pastors are given a weighty and important task. They are to do what is best for the local church and not for their own family. Pastor/shepherds are to sleep out at night with the sheep, feed them first, defend them always; if not, the flock suffers. The pastor/shepherd is committed to long-term care not just as an administrator but as a servant and the steward of the spiritual realities in Christ. Pastors are to be:

- Shepherds and servants, not managers (CEOs).

- Preachers, not lecturers. The sheep need the finest of wheat and anointed exhortations.

- Leaders, not priests. Not 'evangelical priests'!

- Elders must not become lords/kings. The apostle Peter makes this very clear: 'Shepherd the flock of God which is among you, serving as overseers, not by compulsion but willingly, not for dishonest gain but eagerly; nor as being lords over those entrusted to you, but being examples to the flock' (1 Peter 5:2–3).

---

17 **Steward:** n a person who manages and superintends another's affairs, *esp.* an estate; the person who oversees [the] responsible; an overseer; one who serves as a steward. This individual's function in the practical work of the Christian church involves an obligation to give a share of his or her time and goods to others. A Lord High Steward is one of the great officers of state, and the first officer of the crown. (©,cf Chambers Harrap Publishers Ltd: The Chambers Dictionary 2003; The Chambers Thesaurus 2004).

- Examples in faith and life and not as politicians. Hebrews 13:7 and 17 make it clear that the pastor's theology is their guide ('whose faith follow'), but some men want to control the conscience and rule as legislators, not accepting New Testament church polity.

Pastors are to lead by love, serve by love, listen with love and discipline with loving care. They are also to do the work of an evangelist aiming for conversions (2 Timothy 4:5), upholding gospel truth and preaching holy living as God commands. Luther's three qualifications for a pastor are a good guide for us: *(i)* prayer, *(ii)* meditation and *(iii)* suffering! Augustine of Hippo says they are *(i)* humility, *(ii)* humility and *(iii)* humility!

A pastor's trials

Satanic attacks are to be expected. These comprise

(i) attacks on his wife and children. The pastors' wives face criticism and hypocritical opposition and they suffer from this more severely when it is against their husbands. Thus a disciplined and regular prayer life together is very important. Their children need to be shielded from fear and upset.

(ii) Personal feelings toward others! This sensitivity needs to be controlled. I am gregarious by temperament and not easily irritated; however, when grievously hurt bitterness must be avoided—sadly I think only a few (if any) are spared that trial—Spurgeon was not.

(iii) Attacks from without. I would think that today's young pastors will have more of these than I did because of social media and because of the moral downgrade in our society today.

(iv) Criticisms from within the local church. These are the hardest to cope with and especially if you are criticised personally and a deacon or an elder is involved. A word of caution here: if someone in your leaders' meeting says something like, 'I have had a complaint,' it is important that you ask straight away, 'From whom?' If they say, 'I cannot tell you

(saying) it was private and confidential,' you as the chairman must *not* allow it to proceed. It is very important that you are able to place the issue in the context of *the* person or persons involved and their situation. A firm hand is required on this so as to act biblically. Arrogance is not the issue here but clarity and openness with grace.

(*v*) *Satanic attacks* are spasmodic unless there has been a head of steam built up because of neglect in handling things well. However, it is important also to 'live above' the attacks without ignoring their context and importance or non-importance. I found that in the church meetings people in the main only want to make *their* point while respecting the pastor at the same time. But the devil will exaggerate all problem issues so as to cause division. Satan's supreme activity is upon the mind of man. 1 Timothy 4:1 makes it clear: 'Now the Spirit expressly says that in latter times some will depart from the faith, giving heed to deceiving spirits and doctrines of demons.' Satan will try to tell you at times that everyone is against you when it is only one person or two who are the agitators and grumblers. This is one of the first lessons I had to absorb during my years in part-time and full-time ministry (following my induction in 1977).

(*vi*) *Depression.* I have little experience personally of prolonged spells and only a few of my parishioners had it in strong measure. Suffering in all its varieties is the pastor's lot in this fallen world. The New Testament teaches suffering is a harbinger to future blessings and it is not, as atheists say, useless. Job teaches us this, also Paul (2 Corinthians 1:3–11; cf. Hebrews 6:9–12).

Suffering and sanctification

Job was a godly man with a godly way of life. He feared God and shunned evil (1:8b) and, like Noah, he had found grace in the eyes of the Lord (Genesis 6:8), and through the process of his trials and the debate set out in the Book of Job he was helped with the doctrine of God and the difficult problem of human depression and 'undeserved' suffering and his strong faith pulled him through: 'Though He slay me, yet will I trust Him' (Job 13:15). The answer to the question, 'Why suffering?' is not dealt with directly in the Book of Job and that is why no clear answer or obvious reasons are given, but the process of sanctification of God's people is their ordained lot and blessing (Philippians 1:6). Suffering is not a cruel providence as some will contend but mercy and grace calculated to overcome the problem of loneliness, pride, stubbornness and hardness of heart in order that we draw, by faith, closer to Christ and His likeness. Through his trials and pains, Job found what the renewed inner man longs for, viz. a clearer view of God and deeper fellowship with Him. Believers often ask God to draw them closer, or to humble them (not recommended!), or to take them deeper in the Christian life, only to complain when He does so! Job, in the fellowship of Christ's sufferings, confessed, 'I have heard of You by the hearing of the ear, but now my eye sees You. Therefore I abhor myself, and repent in dust and ashes' (Job 42:5–6). Job's religious experience reminds us that God intends us to 'move on with Him' and not remain as babes in Christ. Suffering is not useless or without reason but rather it is the indication of the love of Christ to us (Hebrews 12:5–6). Suffering usually takes us unawares; at least we do not expect its severity.

Do we benefit from the sanctifying process? Robert Murray M'Cheyne often prayed that God would sanctify his trials to him: 'I often pray, Lord, make me as holy as a pardoned sinner can be made.'[18] Suffering never comes alone for it is always followed by the consolations of Christ (2 Corinthians 1:5), i.e. comfort from and by Holy Spirit and the Word. 'Providence not only undertakes but perfects what concerns us. It goes through with its designs and accomplishes what it begins. Its motions are irresistible and incontrollable; God performs it for us (Psalm 57:2). Providence is universal, effectual, beneficial and an encouraging influence upon the affairs and concerns of God's people. It has its eye upon everything

---

18 Quoted, *God Makes a Path*, ed. Stanley Barnes (Belfast: Ambassador, 1997), p.?

that relates to them throughout their lives, from the first to last. It neither does nor can do anything that is really against the true interest and good of the people of God.'[19] We need to look to Christ always in times of trouble (Hebrews 12:1f). In the life of our Lord Jesus Christ His suffering preceded His glorification and so it must be in the life of the child of God; the believer must share in Christ's sufferings.

The work which His goodness began,
The arm of His strength will complete;
His promise is Yea and Amen,
And never was forfeited yet.

(Augustus M. Toplady)

Why suffering?

Since the Fall all pain, disease and death find their origin there. When Adam sinned the whole of creation fell and his failure brought death and suffering into the whole world (Romans 5:12,14). Perhaps some might think that the answer is too religious or too simplistic, but there is no better explanation either in philosophy or theology. If one is inclined to blame God for death and suffering and if God comes into the equation at all, then His own explanation is surely best of all. The book of Genesis tells us all our problems can be traced back to the Fall in Eden's garden (Genesis 3). Suffering can awaken the soul to God and the danger of hell fire ahead. God can take failure and turn it into success. So there is a second reason for all our suffering, namely that through it we seek God's grace and help. Suffering in whatever form gives one the opportunity to turn to God for help; the alternative is to turn against God. Thus, suffering either humbles or hardens. Perhaps we need to stop fighting God and simply and trustingly look to Him for peace, grace and new hope. It is

---

19 John Flavel, *The Mystery of Providence* (Edinburgh: Banner of truth Trust, 1985), pp. 18–19.

there to be found through Jesus Christ His Son (John 14:1,27). There are some things we just cannot explain.

In his book *When Heaven is Silent*, Ronald Dunn tells the story of how he escaped death when a man with a gun robbed him in a motel car park. The robber pushed him over and fired his gun intending to shoot him. The bullet missed and struck the pavement just beside his head. Later he said that God must have been protecting him that day. Yet, not long before, intruders shot two of his friends to death in their own home. Why did God not protect them? The question haunted him. This is what we call 'the Big Why?' God's ways are not our way, so there are some things we just cannot explain except we take into account the fall of man into sin, because this has brought suffering and death into the world. Due to the consequences of the fall there are some things which will not be changed or rectified until eternity. But there is help. God has promised that things will change for the better and He 'will wipe away every tear from their eyes; there shall be no more death, nor sorrow, nor crying. There shall be no more pain' (Revelation 21:4). Is "Why?" the right question? Surely, it would be better to ask, 'What now?' Perhaps things have changed, and we must take stock. To ask, 'What now?' breaks the cycle of anger, depression and self-pity we feel. 'What now?' ushers in new hope and shifts our focus from ourselves to God and what He is up to in our lives. God only wants the best for us. We must believe that and trust Him for the future. 'Through the Lord's mercies we are not consumed, because His compassions fail not. They are new every morning; great is Your faithfulness (Lamentations 3:22–23).

The pastor's spiritual battle

The constant spiritual battles that pastors have require them to be always in the Spirit and always watching out for the devil's devices. This is a dimension that pastors inhabit and is not the ordinary daily life of members or what he encountered before ordination. Christian ministry is something out of the ordinary and necessitates daily holiness and constant watching and praying. How blessed pastors are if with faithful wives and loving children they keep the faith. Timothy is commanded to commit Paul's teachings to heart and share it with faithful men who will teach others (2 Timothy 2:1–4). There is also an instruction to stay unchanging in calling and be steadfast in aim even in times of 'hardship' (Greek *kakopatheia*, i.e. 'suffering and ill treatment').[20] Pastors and believers are to bear up under trials, adversity, hardship and suffering which may entail poverty and deprivation of liberty:

You therefore must *endure hardship* as a good soldier of Jesus Christ. No one engaged in warfare entangles himself with the affairs of this life, that he may please him who enlisted him as a soldier. (2 Timothy 2:3–4)

Compare:

'*I suffer* trouble as an evildoer, even to the point of chains; but the word of God is not chained' (2 Timothy 2:8).

The spiritual struggle must not be weakened by worldly interests, distractions and occupations. Many pastors have ignored this instruction, resulting in weakened usefulness and witness. Three helpful illustrations are given to explain pastoral vocation in 2 Timothy 2. 'The first is a soldier; the Christian walk is often presented as spiritual warfare: effective service calls for singleness of purpose. The second illustration comes from athletics: no competitor could be crowned unless he competed in accordance with the rules. Faithful pastors will receive a victor's crown [cf. Revelation 2:10]. The third illustration is that of a hardworking farmer: conscientious, hard labour is necessary before a farmer can enjoy a bountiful harvest. Laziness must not be a character trait of Christ's under-shepherds.'[21]

---

20 Greek, 'I am ill-treated'; Souter, *A Pocket Lexicon*.
21 Nelson CD_ROM, adapted.

Conclusion

The call to a local church will dictate your scope of service and the tasks necessary to being a blessing to God's people who have called you in faith and look to you for leadership. Pray that you will not let them down. A day off is essential: perhaps two! I did not require more than one in the Lord's goodness and providential care. It is necessary to come apart and rest a while, but not to waste time. The build-up to the Lord's Day is always very busy and worship is the main event each week, and so a day off is recommended. Faithfulness and a 'well done' is always our goal. Perseverance is necessary in one's calling and spiritual and social gifts are required, but no one man has them all! The fear of man can be a snare and so the fear of God is the antidote. Spurgeon's pastoral leadership approach to church government with his deacons was wise; however, today it looks more authoritarian and some church leaders are into 'heavy shepherding'.[22] It is always good to remember that the man of God is an under-shepherd who answers first to his Saviour Jesus Christ. Like Jesus he is tasked with caring for the sheep, i.e. those church members on his appointed roll.

Praying (intercession) is what Jesus is doing *now*, i.e. making intercession for us. What He promised Peter He promises all the people of God: 'I have prayed for you, that your faith should not fail,' because He *is* now in heaven praying for us at the right hand of the throne on high (Luke 22:32; Hebrews 7:25). He represents us there as our 'Advocate with the Father'. Peter had a mighty friend at the right hand of God. Ryle says: 'There is a watchful Advocate, who is daily pleading for him, seeing all his daily necessities, and obtaining daily supplies of mercy and grace for his soul.'[23] The Lord Jesus prophesied and counselled at the same time: 'When you

---

22 Those leaders of churches who become involved in the minute details of people's personal lives at a highly controlling level (e.g. in areas of money and relationships and more) will seek to control the conscience.

23 J.C. Ryle, *Expository Thoughts on the Gospels, St Luke*, Vol. 2 (London: James Clark & Co., 1969), p. 411.

have returned to Me, strengthen your brethren' (Luke 22:32). Peter would backslide, but the prayers of his personal Saviour would be answered and he would return to his first love in a restored and spiritually strengthened manner, and he would continue his ministry and he would also help others to be strong in the Lord and in the power of His might.

Solutions to our trials (I summarise):

1. Tip-top personal daily spirituality.
2. Deal with problems by using the supporting elders' interventions to protect you.
3. Keep to biblical solutions and avoid personal hang-ups.
4. Don't be in a hurry to make important decisions (Proverbs 16:3).
5. Cover everything and everyone in prayer.
6. Be always under the blood of Christ. Repentance and faith must be a daily exercise, while taking up our cross is necessary to follow in the Saviour's footsteps. An awareness of the forgiveness of sins is required and cleansing from all sin is essential (1 John 1:9; 2:1–2). Jesus ever lives to pray for us, and therefore a clear understanding of the doctrine of His heavenly session is very helpful to our perseverance in the ministry (cf. Luke 22:32; cf. Mark 14:38).

3. Pastors are sent *from* God

'Prayer and preaching is the Twelve's calling following [the ascension]. Paul, knowing the power of preaching backed by prayer wrote, "in the church I would rather speak five words with my understanding, that I may teach others also, than ten thousand words in a tongue" (1 Corinthians 14:19). Five words, spoken with humility, authority, tenderness, and love all by the Holy Spirit are full of potential life-transforming power.' (Geoff Thomas)[24]

'The harvest truly is great, but the labourers are few; therefore pray the Lord of the harvest to send out labourers into His harvest. Go your way; behold, I send you out as lambs among wolves.' (Luke 10:2–3)

'There was a man sent from God, whose name was John.' (John 1:6)

Sent preachers are the Lord's messengers speaking the Lord's message; 'Then Haggai, the LORD's messenger, spoke the LORD's message to the people, saying, "I am with you, says the LORD"' (Haggai 1:13). This reality was on Paul's lips when he said to the church in Rome, 'And how shall they preach unless they are sent?' (Romans 10:15). Our Lord's high priestly prayer made this an item in prayer: 'I do not pray for these alone, but also for those who will believe in Me through their word' (John 17:20). God's messengers are those who are sent and are ambassadors charged to speak of Him and His kingdom:

---

24 Geoff Thomas, 'A Fresh Look at Basics', The Banner of Truth Magazine No. 693, June 2021.

We are ambassadors for Christ, as though God were pleading through us: we implore you on Christ's behalf, be reconciled to God. (2 Corinthians 5:20)

Pastors are men who speak for and from God and they cannot afford to be afraid of men (or women!) with their vociferous and fickle opinions. Paul was of such an attitude:

Do I now persuade men, or God? Or do I seek to please men? For if I still pleased men, I would not be a bondservant of Christ. (Galatians 1:10)

God still sends today

Preaching is a pastor's calling. The called pastor is a man sent from God and as an under-shepherd he teaches the sheep and the lambs, as confirmed by Jesus's words to Peter:

He said to him, 'Feed My lambs.' He said to him again a second time, 'Simon, son of Jonah, do you love Me?' He said to Him, 'Yes, Lord; You know that I love You.' He said to him, 'Tend My sheep.' (John 21:15–16)

As God's messenger the pastor/preacher is to be a contender for righteousness and the faith given to the saints. He is to manage the church (with his fellow elders' help) because it is 'the pillar and ground of the truth' (1 Timothy 3:15). All this adds up to a holy calling and sanctified ministry, a profession and a way of life. Not every believer is called or gifted or expected to be the Lord's messenger, with the Lord's message to the Lord's people. That is because it is a vocation and men who have that calling are to be sought out as pastors for our churches. While there are good brothers who can minister the Word and may get a turn at speaking from time to time—and some do well—our congregations are to be led by those with a high and holy calling who commit themselves to that service as a life's work in the Lord's 'army'. They are to:

Be watchful in all things, endure afflictions, do the work of an evangelist, fulfil your ministry. (2 Timothy 4:5)

Part-time ministries are unable to 'be watchful in all things' as other responsibilities take up their time and energy. Fulfilling full-time ministry demands courage, as well as faith; strength as well as will; anointing as well as education; calling as well as the new birth; time as well as ambition. I am convinced that good men have missed out on having more successful ministries by failing to more seriously take up their cross and forget about their pension! Life is too short to miss out on the privilege to preach full-time and to call many to repentance. When Paul speaks of being sent to preach God's Word it was seen as a special calling for him. This he states while in prison in Rome; he wrote that God:

manifested His word through preaching, which was committed *to me* according to the commandment of God our Saviour. (Titus 1:3) [25]

The phrase 'manifested His word through preaching' explains that from eternity God promised eternal life through the covenant of grace which ('in due time') was made clear and obvious by preaching the gospel to the world of both Jews and Gentiles 'in hope of eternal life which God, who cannot lie, promised before time began' (Titus 1:2; cf. Genesis 3:15; Psalm 32:1–2a; Romans 1:17; Ephesians 3:4–5; 1 Timothy 2:6; 6:15; Galatians 4:4). The phrase, 'preaching, which was committed to me', tells us that the gospel would be revealed and understood through a public religious discourse by a spokesman for God. Redemption's mysteries were not fully realised or proclaimed by the prophets of the Old Testament (Romans 16:25–26; Colossians 1:26a; Habakkuk 2:4; Joel 2:28–29, etc.), so Paul and his successors were divinely authorised and commissioned to do that. It is 'through preaching' that we hear, learn and believe the gospel of

---

25 My emphasis.

Jesus Christ. Lloyd-Jones puts it thus: 'The first business of the preacher of salvation is to call men to repentance' (*The Righteous Judgment of God*, p. 145).[26]

To preach is 'to herald', not in weakness but in God's strength to proclaim the salvation of God as an ambassador of the Most High. Pastors are men speaking for, from and about God. The world will not do that. The schoolteacher rarely tells. Only those who are called and only those are sent will pay the price and do the work for little earthly reward. To preach is what the pastors have to do, so as to 'tell it as it is' by preaching the whole counsel of God in Christ. They are to teach and encourage faith in those who will listen and even those who will not (2 Timothy 4:2). Without gifts, calling and training it cannot be done well or as well as it might.

How shall they believe in Him of whom they have not heard? ... And how shall they preach unless they are sent? (Romans 10:14)

We need to take heed to what is written or we will get the wrong men in the pulpit and the wrong persons in the ministries of God. Prayer is necessary to ask for the best of men to pastor the local flocks of God. We are to ask God to send us His herald, which is about calling and sending not only to the mission fields but to pulpits at home (Luke 10:2).

Why ask God to send them? Because it is a calling and commission and not professionalism in its secular sense but an inner personal sense of duty and responsibility given by the Spirit and being accountable to Jesus Christ our Lord, and because no one will do it unless God sends them! If they do go from any other motive they will not outlast the call. Preachers are sent as lambs among wolves (Luke 10:3). Those who are called are given the special grace of calling. The martyrs had 'dying grace' and the front-line soldiers of the Lord are equipped with a special anointing to work through 'thick and thin' for God's glory and Jesus' joy. Jesus' words in Luke 10

26 Quoted, Sargent, *Gems from Martyn Lloyd-Jones*, p.231.

are set in the context of need and duty and thus Jesus asks for prayer to be made for labourers to be sent to work in the world's harvest fields so that many will believe, for 'faith comes by *hearing*, and hearing by the word of God' (Romans 10:17).

Pastors are to be as the oracle of Jesus Christ, i.e. persons that speak with the authority of the Word of God in the power of the Holy Spirit. Preaching holds a great responsibility towards God and pastors *must avoid the errors and attitudes of Balaam*. Balaam is associated with greed and is guilty of promoting fornication (2 Peter 2:15; Jude 11; Revelation 2:14). He may at first appear to have feared God and be His messenger, but this was not so and the risen Jesus Christ clarifies that in Revelation 2:14. Balaam's words to King Balak, 'Must I not take heed to speak what the LORD has put in my mouth?' (Numbers 23:11–12), may sound good: but not so! Twice more he claims that God would not let him speak falsely against Israel. How could a false prophet act that way? The New Testament has an example of prophecy spoken by an unsaved man (John 11:49–52). In Joshua 13:22, Balaam is called a soothsayer, i.e. a predictor of the future. Balaam's services were for hire apparently; something similar was taking place in the church at Pergamos, especially in regard to idols and sexual immorality (Revelation 2:14). Here we see an example that 'the heart is deceitful above all things, and desperately wicked' (Jeremiah 17:9).

Pastors' appointed tasks

Today there are many enemies and increasing opposition to the evangelical Christian protestant religion. You may be aware of it in the media; even the *London Times* is boldly speaking out against the Christian faith.[27] Pastors, as the guardians of the faith, are to speak out against apostasy and theological error (1 Timothy 3:16; 2 Timothy 2:15; Jude 3).

---

27 Matthew Parris, a columnist, was allowed to pontificate: 'Friends, there are no demons, no Heaven, no Hell, no cosmic forces of good and evil, no battle between darkness and light. There is only us', (Saturday, January 1, 2022).

When it comes to the local church, God sends His servants to aid, encourage and lead into blessing. God's aid came to Israel by raising up Samuel the prophet. This is how He works with His people today still. There is hope in Jesus who was sent from heaven, viz., God's Son our Redeemer, and aid from the Holy Spirit our Guide; and His Word our light which comes to us by those called and committed to preach. We are not to 'despise prophesyings' (1 Thessalonians 5:20). 'By the term *prophesying*, I mean the science of the interpretation of Scripture. The statement is remarkable for its commendation for outward preaching.'[28] The true prophets and preachers know God and speak for God:

We are of God. He who knows God hears us; he who is not of God does not hear us. By this we know the spirit of truth and the spirit of error. (1 John 4:6)

Pastors' words are not their own but Christ's and His Spirit's. The pastors' aim is not to please men but God; their task is to speak the whole council of God, in season and out of season, the Holy Spirit helping them; they exalt the person and work of Jesus Christ, taking nothing away; they must decrease but Jesus Christ must increase.

Isaiah[29] is a great example of God working and speaking to His elect people and the nations around about Israel. God mediates His message through Isaiah to Israel and Judah (the people of the southern kingdom) and specifically to their magistrates, priests, and prophets in Jerusalem. Isaiah speaks prophetic *words of warning*, but he also records *words of promise* and hope. This is the task appointed to every New Testament pastor. Isaiah spoke of the coming Messiah: 'Zion shall be redeemed with justice, and her penitents with righteousness' and he spoke (prophesied) of the destiny of the church of God (Isaiah 1:27; 40:1 – 66:24; cf. Galatians 2:21;

---

28 John Calvin, The Banner of Truth Magazine, Nov. 2002, p. 12.
29 Isaiah ('the Lord is salvation'), prophesied for 63 years between 739 and 686 BC and saw the nation of Assyria take the northern kingdom into captivity in 722 BC.

Philippians 3:9) bringing hope, and he preached the Messiah's salvation, comfort, and blessings (61:1–3; Luke 4:17–19). Here again we see the responsibility of those who are called to pastor and preach Jesus Christ and Him crucified and risen again on the third day. As Christian pastors we are to recognise that our religion in not man-made but rather a God-ordained faith. Thus there are God's Word and the Holy Spirit (who seals us) to help His remnant people in these latter days and who provides by giving His churches His overseers (elders):

1. These pastors are called and fitted for service in their local settings.

2. These men assist local churches by the preaching of the gospel in the power of the Spirit.

3. These brothers in the Lord aid evangelism and church growth in due time.

4. These pastors serve local churches through the ministry of the two sacraments: baptism and communion.

Called to learn

There was no requirement for training for ministry in the early church. However, in the New Testament it is clear that a call to preach was paramount if God's blessing is to follow (Romans 10:14–15). Early on, as the office of bishop/teachers developed in the second and third centuries there was some instruction for new candidates and Origen (c. 184–c. 253) established a school in Alexandria. Later Augustine of Hippo established what would become 'The Canons of Saint Augustine'. These Institutes included a bibliography of recommended reading: the singing of Psalms, schools of grammar, astronomy and rhetoric, logic, geometry, arithmetic and music were set up. Finally there was the study of Scripture itself, including theology, and pastoral ministry. Leaders and elders instructed new and potential clergy. The advent of scholasticism in the twelfth century led to the establishment of universities. At the Reformation, Melanchthon and Bullinger insisted on the importance of theological education and the School of Theology in Geneva was particularly significant. Here Calvin produced his *Institutes of Religion*, but also a catechism for lay people. In the Academy led by Theodore Beza there was the scholarly learning and teaching of Latin, French and Greek, and then the more advanced teaching of theology and exegesis. In 1564 there were 1,200 students; these were the missionaries who would take the gospel to the Netherlands, Scotland and England, where similar schools would be established. Roman Catholic practice and theology needed to be countered by a clearer biblical understanding.[30]

We see that the importance of training for ministry is historically led. But now the challenge of present day secular university culture makes it imperative to train men not only by imparting information but by giving and encouraging piety as well as learning. C. H. Spurgeon was aware of the dangers of the enlightenment and rationalism combined with liberal theology in a university education so that he (wisely) set up a church-based academy, providing not only instruction but a model of healthy and fruitful church life and ministry. The tutors of his college were often not only scholars but also recognised elders in the church. Many of the students lodged with families in the church. Closer to home Dr Martyn Lloyd-Jones was concerned about theological education in the universities, and that English Free Church men were training at Anglican colleges. Hence he wanted the teaching not to be merely academic but to promote the personal knowledge of God.[31] Some autodidactic men are found in church history but they are not the majority. The apostles from

---

30 Help found in: Justo Gonzalez, *The History of Theological Education* (Routledge: Abingdon, 2015).
31 D. Martyn Lloyd-Jones, London Theological Seminary public lecture, October 1977.

the beginning were taught by the Saviour Himself. Pastors need to think deeply, but also they need to be alert to the possibility of neglecting the practice of preaching and the needed goal of reaching the hordes of the lost around us who are to hear the Good News (Romans 10:14–15).

4. The pastor's vision

'The pastor can employ no means more certain to sanctify his flock than reading and reflecting upon their part.' (W. G. T. Shedd) [32]

'The pastor is a man who is given charge of souls. He is not merely a nice, pleasant man who visits people. He is the guardian, the custodian, the protector, the organiser, the director, the ruler of the flock.' (D. Martyn Lloyd-Jones, *Christian Unity*, p. 193) [33]

'We are commanded to take heed to all the flock, it is plainly implied, that flocks must ordinarily be no greater than we are capable of overseeing, or "taking heed to".' (Richard Baxter) [34]

'He Himself gave some to be apostles, some prophets, some evangelists, and some pastors and teachers, for the equipping of the saints for the work of ministry, for the edifying of the body of Christ, till we all come to the unity of the faith and of the knowledge of the Son of God, to a perfect man, to the measure of the stature of the fullness of Christ.' (Ephesians 4:11–13)

Y ou will notice in Ephesians 4:11–13 that the apostle speaks about unity. He speaks of a unity of which the Holy Spirit is the author. This exists where the true church is found and Charles Hodge

---

32 W. G. T. Shedd, *Homiletics & and Pastoral Theology* (London: The Banner of Truth Trust, 1965), p. 285.
33 Quoted, Sargent, *Gems from Martyn Lloyd-Jones*, p. 212.
34 Richard Baxter, *The Reformed Pastor* (Edinburgh: The Banner of Truth Trust, 1979), p. 88.

says: 'The exhortation is that the greatest zeal should be exercised in its preservation', and he continues that Paul 'labours to bring the Jewish and Gentile Christians to this spirit of mutual forbearance'.[35] The way to do this is given in verse 2; here we have the graces of meekness, love and longsuffering as the keys to success. They are an equal trio of 'essential oils' wholly necessary if the fragrance of the Holy Spirit is to linger long in the house of God. In Ephesians we see that God gives gifts to hold the churches together. These are ascension gifts from the risen and ruling Christ to His church: 'When He ascended on high, He led captivity captive, and gave gifts to men' (Ephesians 4:8).

God gives gifts

Christ has provided gifted persons necessary to serve His kingdom on earth for the local churches' benefit and edification; they are listed for us:

Firstly, *apostles*—they were the teachers of the church, who personally witnessed the resurrection (Ephesians 2:20) and we see they are the foundation of Christendom with the Saviour. There are no apostles alive today, for in its strict sense it refers only to those who saw Jesus Christ perform His miracles, witnessed His bodily resurrection and were specially chosen by Christ to tell others about Himself from their eyewitness accounts (cf. John 17:12ff). This allows the readers to embrace apostolic teaching (a foundation is laid once only so there is no need for more apostles or prophets or other revelation). *Apostles* also means (in a Bible context) 'envoys' or 'ambassadors' who are preachers and teachers in apostolic succession having the 66 books of the canon of Scripture in a vernacular form as well as in the original autographs.

Secondly, *prophets* were those who received and spoke by divine inspiration (Ephesians 3:5). They delivered direct revelations from God before the New Testament was written (cf. 1 Corinthians 14). They

---

35 Charles Hodge, *Ephesians* (London: The Banner of Truth Trust, 1964), p.20.

foretold God's actions in the future, and they proclaimed what God had already said in the Old Testament Scriptures.

Thirdly, *evangelists* were God's missionary preachers sent to preach the gospel and plant churches. They are gospel preachers who through gospel ministry bring people into the local (church) body of Christ and also train believers to share their faith effectively among others.

Fourthly, *pastors and teachers* are one holy office, pastors being the under-shepherds of the Lord's redeemed people, who are by them to be fed, nurtured and protected from evil enemies. If a shepherd does what he is supposed to do, he will have healthy sheep and lambs and his flock will grow. The two Koine Greek nouns and their context tie the two titles *teachers* and *pastors* closely together in one office. There is a tension between the role of pastor and evangelist, however; the pastor/teacher is to do the 'work of the evangelist' (2 Timothy 4:5), while called to be an under-shepherd to feed, nurture and protect Christ's sheep. The evangelist will preach, exhort, advise, counsel as he church plants with a passion for souls. He may need to seek out a church that will finance him and that will not stand in the way of the evangelist who needs to step out in faith and trust the Lord as the Holy Spirit leads (cf. Acts 11:25).

A pastor's goal

A local church pastor/teacher is to achieve two goals:

The first is to 'the equipping of the saints for the work of ministry' (Ephesians 4:12, Greek *diakonia*, i.e. 'to make one what he ought to be', Thayer) and by steady progress 'to make fit' and 'to prepare fully'. Therefore, as the KJV, 'perfecting of the saints', or as the NIV, 'to prepare God's people'. The model described is bringing to excellence the athlete who is to be neither flabby nor sluggish but to be in peak condition and ready for the race before him. For Hodge it is 'that service which one man renders to another'.[36]

---

36 Ibid. p. 228.

The second goal is 'the edifying of the body of Christ' (Greek *oikodomē*, edifying), i.e. 'building up' by feeding and nourishing it. Is this the reason the churches are so weak today? The emphasis on sacraments and liturgy is one thing, but it has weakened the authority of Bible preaching and teaching through sermons. If no authoritative word is given and no objective truth is believed then no strong and faithful witnesses are produced. It is clear from this passage that such perfecting takes time when preparing the saints to be fit to run the heavenly race (Hebrews 12:1b–2). Thus commitment from both pastor and people working in agreement is required.

Paul's stress is growth from unity with every member working together in 'the body for the edifying of itself in love' (4:16). He is concerned not only that Christians should know but also that Christians should grow. For some congregations that will only happen as the pastor grows with it. God is concerned not with size but with the quality of spiritual health and growth. Those engaged in pastoral ministry are exhorted to 'walk worthy of their calling' and to forbear with all those who are under their leadership with care and love. It is obvious here that Paul was conscious of the physical and mental strain that is common in pastoral work; he speaks of 'bearing [Greek *anechomai*] with one another': it implies the need to 'endure' in times of frustration or conflict (lit. 'to hold up', cf. 2 Thessalonians 1:4; 3:3). It involves the exercising of spiritual graces in continuous flowing blessings; as he exhorts:

Walk worthy of the calling with which you were called, with all lowliness and gentleness, with longsuffering, bearing [*anechomenoi*] with one another in love, endeavouring to keep the unity of the Spirit in the bond of peace. (Ephesians 4:1–3)

Pastoral graces

Three graces are evident in the practical care of God's sheep:

'**Lowliness**', rather, 'humility' (Greek *tapeinophrosunē*) of mind. In Acts 20:19 Paul acknowledges this was his practice with modesty in mind and approach in service among God's people. This follows in the Apostle's and Christ's footsteps: 'Let nothing be done through selfish ambition or conceit, but in lowliness of mind let each esteem others better than himself. Let each of you look out not only for his own interests, but also for the interests of others' (Philippians 2:3–4). This latter encouragement (v. 4) calls for self-sacrifice in all aspects of the pastor's living.

'Gentleness', rather, meekness (Greek *praotēs*). Paul is speaking of a relationship with the people of God, and thus a man-ward horizontal connection sourced from a gracious and given meekness is necessary. Meekness before God is also a prerequisite for shepherding the flock of God because the under-shepherd must display the fruit of the Spirit in ministry and service knowing that he must give an account (James 3:1). Meekness is that spirit which accepts God's dealings with us as good while laying aside our self-will by accepting God's providence without stubbornness or bitterness (think on Job, or Jacob). It is Christlikeness: remember His words, 'Not My will, but Yours, be done.' The Holy Spirit is the source of this 'fruit of the Spirit' and He will grant to us this grace of meekness also. So, living in the Spirit, let pastors also walk in the Spirit (Ephesians 4:23–24). In other words, with meekness there is acquiescing:

- *To God's will:* as with Eli when Samuel told him what the Lord said regarding his sons, he replied: 'It is the LORD, let Him do what seems good to Him' (1 Samuel 3:18). This submission acknowledges that God is Lord. Jonah was the opposite of meek—he responded: 'It is right for me to be angry!' (Jonah 4:9).

- *To God's way:* Joseph was called to walk a difficult and lonely path in Egypt and is a good example of sanctified meekness. Moses too is a good example of one who was meek (read Numbers 12:3). He put up with many injuries, but 'instead of falling into a rage, he fell into prayer', said Thomas Watson (cf. Exodus 15:24–25).

- *To God's Word:* meekness is being willing to let the Word bear sway in one's souls, conforming oneself to the mind of God and not quarrelling with the instructions of the Word of God. The example of our Saviour is paramount when it comes to meekness. He did not quarrel with the Word of God in the Old Testament Scriptures but He yielded to its prophecies: thus He received Judas's kiss; He went to the cross as the lamb to the slaughter; He said, 'I am meek and lowly in heart' (Matthew 11:29).

To the world *meekness* is weakness, yet nothing could be further from the truth as it is in fact an inner power and a calm serenity. Only the strong spiritual believer can be truly meek. 'Meekness' is having the resources of God at your disposal. It is having power to take insults and injuries without retaliation. It is the power to be courteous and considerate and really mean it and, as R. C. Trench says, 'Meekness consists not in a person's outward behaviour; nor in his relationship to his fellow man … it is an inwrought grace in the soul.'[37] We can now see that 'meekness' is an inward attitude of the heart and can be translated as gentleness as that is its outward action reflecting the grace in a sanctified believer. Meekness is a badge of honour for the Christian. Sadly, however, it is despised by the world, tasteless to the old nature and undervalued by the people of God.

'Longsuffering' is a compound word—*makrothumia*, from *makros*, 'long', and *thumia*, 'temper', therefore 'long-temper' and thus 'longsuffering', i.e. 'slowness in avenging wrongs'. This does not go quite as far as the New Testament requires of the believer but it points in the right direction. W. E. Vine says that 'longsuffering is that quality of self-restraint in the face of provocation which does not hastily retaliate or promptly punish. It is the opposite of anger and it is associated with mercy'.[38] 'Longsuffering' is a quality of self-restraint especially under trying circumstances (note that the Holy Spirit is a Spirit of self-control, 2 Timothy 1:7). W. Hendriksen

37 R. C. Trench, *Synonyms of the New Testament* (p. xlii).
38 W. E. Vine, *Expository Dictionary of Bible Words* (London: Marshall Morgan & Scott, 1985).

reckons 'it characterises the person who in relation to those who annoy, oppose or molest him, exercises patience. He refuses to yield to passion or outburst of anger'.[39] The NIV translates the Greek as *patience* but the KJV and NKJV as *longsuffering*, and the latter is best because patience (*hupomonē*) speaks of endurance with regard to things and circumstances, while *longsuffering* is patience with regards to adverse people! A man is patient having no choice but to bear with his problems and be longsuffering under trial as was Job who had no choice but waited for God to intervene and undertake in answer to his prayers. For Alexander Souter, patience is 'steadfast endurance, the virtue shown by martyrs'.[40] John Chrysostom says longsuffering (*makrothumia*) 'is a man having power to avenge himself, yet refrains from exercising that power'. Longsuffering is a person refraining from retaliation, like Joseph when his guilty brothers stood before him in Egypt (Genesis 45). He could act against them but he does not. Love kept his anger at bay. 'Lowliness and gentleness, with longsuffering', are combined by the Spirit here to emphasise the nature of pastoral ministry and its challenges. The pastor is to speak the truth in love (Ephesians 4:15) so that the saints may grow up in all things into Him who is the head of the church: Jesus Christ. A teacher speaks the truth, but a pastor must speak the truth in love, not just cold doctrine and information, nor the letter of law to rule with legal enforcement, but with love—always love (1 Corinthians 16:13–14). A pastor is tasked to help, support, protect, and to care as Christ's under-shepherd, depending always on the need of personal spiritual graces from the Holy Spirit (cf. Galatians 5:16–26).

Conclusion

The equipping of the saints for the work of ministry is a means to an end, viz. 'the edifying of the body of Christ' (Ephesians 4:12) in order to gain a

---

39 W. Hendriksen, *Galatians* (Edinburgh: The Banner of Truth Trust, 1981), p. 224.
40 Alexander Souter, *A Pocket Lexicon to the Greek New Testament*, (Oxford: Clarendon Press, 1960).

unity that is of God (4:3). So pastoral ministry has a timeless purpose, i.e. the growth of the church both spiritually and doctrinally, aiming at amity established by gospel truth and mature love.

The growth of the church is taught here. The church illustrated as a body is to grow, and like a child it will have growing pains, and like the adolescent learning curves as well as troubles are recognised until it attains to 'the measure of the stature of the fullness of Christ' (v. 13). When it comes to body life the pastor has his own special place and function. The position of each part of the body is not self-determined but placed there by the Christ Himself. The mature believer acknowledges and accepts this. The mention of gifts reminds us that we all have not the same task and function, for our gifts vary. The eye does not say to the feet, 'You should be doing what I am doing!' We do what our gifts allow. If we attempt more then we will fail, and if we don't recognise this we may become bitter. We must do our part and fulfil our function; this is what Christ has placed us in the body to do. Growing up has three parts to it: (1) 'till we all come to the unity of the faith', which is the appropriation of His love and looking to Christ only for grace and salvation: He is our object of faith; (2) to 'the knowledge of the Son of God', which is the apprehension of His glory, viz. His eternal Sonship, high priesthood and kingship; (3) 'to a perfect man', which is the appearing of a holy church. Unity is imperfect now, so the ascended Christ at the right hand of the majesty on high is interceding still until the finish is reached (Hebrews 7:25).

5. Pastoral care

'Do not wait until strength and understanding have left them, but go to them as soon as you hear they are sick—do not wait for them to send for you.' (Richard Baxter)[41]

'Those sins that have been committed before all must be reproved before all, that all may fear. Reprove in secret those who offend you in secret. For if you alone know the guilty person, yet you desire to reprove them before others, then you are not a corrector but a betrayer.' (Richard Baxter)[42]

'Sound judgement and solid experience must instruct you: gentle manners and loving affections must sway you; firmness and courage must be manifest; and tenderness and sympathy must not be lacking.' (C. H. Spurgeon)[43]

'Now the man Moses was very meek, above all the men which were upon the face of the earth.' (Numbers 12:3, KJV)

I t has been said that the local pastor is 'a Jack of all trades but a master of none'—at least this is how he may feel at times! Those educated with superior gifts are the speakers at conferences while he, the local pastor, is (just) an ordinary fellow being an exhorter in the Word and in piety. Some men have proficiency in related disciplines such as sociology,

---

41 Richard Baxter, *The Reformed Pastor* (Marshalltown, DE: The National Foundation for Christen Education, no date), p. 19.
42 Richard Baxter, ibid, pp. 20,21.
43 C. H. Spurgeon, *Lectures to My Students*, p. 32.

psychology or medicine while the ordinary pastor may be deficient in these areas and issues of modernity and politics. However, this is not how things are to be viewed remembering that training in theology, doctrinal and pastoral, is recommended to manage people's spiritual needs and wellbeing. We know that Moses was a great leader and pastor to Israel, but he was the meekest of men (Numbers 12:3) and exhibited an inner strength allowing him to cope with all that was expected of him. His striking of the 'Rock' was an uncontrolled moment leaving lasting consequences that could not be changed. Pastoral care requires an understanding of scriptural wisdom, evangelical doctrine and tradition with great helpings of 'lowliness and gentleness, with longsuffering'. I share some of my attempts to reach out and help as the Saviour's under-shepherd.

Divorce and remarriage

This is a controversial subject in evangelical circles but one which every pastor needs to be steady and fixed about in his own mind. Not only so, but a new pastoral candidate for a local evangelical church needs to question the leaders about their position on divorce and remarriage. If that is avoided it is possible that on the first occasion this issue raises its head the church could split! I have known good members leave because of disagreement on divorce and remarriage. All churches, if possible, should have this thought through and their position made clear to all its members. Below I have included a personal letter to two parties whose marriage was in danger of ending.

Dear Friends,

I thought that perhaps I could help you both after hearing that you intend to 'work things out together'. I am so happy about this, this is God's will for you; 'For the LORD God ... says that He hates divorce' (Malachi 2:16a). When your marriage is in difficulty there are things that you must do.

(1) You must seek out competent help. Please *do not* ignore this advice. After the trauma you have both gone through, this is essential for success. Go to your pastor or minister—professional counsellors are okay, but on the whole they do not think biblically so stay clear of them if possible.

(2) You must forgive each other for the problems of the past, only then will you eventually forget them. Paul says in Colossians 3:13, 'bear with one another and forgive one another … even as Christ forgave you, so you also must do'. Start here and stay here; if you do not do this Galatians 5:15 is the result!

(3) You must keep your spiritual lives tip-top. Backsliding is a big factor here and is the cause of much disharmony in Christian marriages. By having strong faith in Christ and a close communion with Him we can meet the difficulties and demands of each day (Galatians 5:16). Remember that the Christian life is a 'series of new beginnings', so come close to Christ again today.

(4) If you have moved out—then move back in together straight away—do not delay, this is very important. The Bible declares man and wife to be *one*, 'they shall become one flesh' (Genesis 2:24), and so it is incongruous that they should be apart. Paul tells us that married couples should separate only for a short time (and with mutual consent) so as to fast and pray then they must come together because Satan is after them! (1 Corinthians 7:5).[44]

(5) You must be determined to work together through a good study book on marriage and relationships such as *(i)* Brian and Barbara Edwards' *No Longer Two* (from Day One Publications) and read chapter 5 especially to begin with; *(ii)* Jay Adams' *Christian Living in the Home* (from Presbyterian and Reformed Publishing). Order them from your local Christian bookshop.

---

44 However, if living together brings on violence (that breaks their marriage vows) then this should not be done until reconciliation is achieved and forgiveness found.

(6) You must re-establish a prayer life together—you are one in Christ, so express this spiritual oneness through devotion together. Set a regular pattern each day, at a time that suits you both, and then it will not be easy to neglect it. Pray together and do so no matter how you feel and take to heart the Bible's advice, 'do not let the sun go down on your wrath' (Ephesians 4:26).

Remember that the best of marriages need to be worked at to remain strong and to make them better. We must give ourselves to each other 100 percent *all* the time; 50–50, is not good enough! When we have given our partners all we can they will always 'demand' more from the relationship. Love needs to be as strong as death for it to work when tested. This is why Paul tells us our relationship in Christ is like a marriage (Ephesians 5:25–32). Unless we give Jesus all He asks of us freely and in obedience our relationship and fellowship will falter. Lastly, I would say there is need for both of you to humble yourselves before God (1 Peter 5:5b–6). If you take the pain of reconciliation now, the joy of love and unity will be yours tomorrow; otherwise short-term 'peace' will prove to be long-term regret. If you take my advice your marriage can be saved. You can then continue your Christian calling together assured of God's grace and help; you and your children will be spared the horror of a divorce and half a lifetime of conflict; and you can know again the joy and blessings of a loving married relationship.

This is my prayer for you both, with my love,

PASTOR.

PS. Check out what these Bible verses say about marriage: Malachi 2:16; Matthew 19:6; 1 Corinthians 7:5; Ephesians 5:25 and 33; 1 Peter 3:7; Hebrews 13:4.

Bereavement and grief

It is in God's plan that we grieve: 'Abraham came to mourn for Sarah and to weep for her' (Genesis 23:2b). Bereavement brings many strong emotions to the surface. These may be a sense of utter worthlessness, absolute despair, guilt, anger, fear, weakness and bitterness. They are not shared by all hurting people but may come and go or ebb and flow in every heart. A sense of relief can be the first response to bereavement, especially when a loved one has had a long illness and a difficult death; this is quite normal and you must not think that it is wrong for you to feel this way. Bereaved persons need to be very patient with themselves and self-pity must be guarded against. The powerful side-effects both emotionally and physically are mostly temporary. Emotional effects are loss of strength, zeal, joy and initiative. Laziness leading to depression can set in. Planning can seem pointless and loneliness is by far the biggest problem. To keep their pain to a minimum some become reserved and distant toward others. It has been known for people to hear voices or see a vision of their loved ones after they have died. Physical effects are also common and feeling unwell is not unusual. The side-effects too are common and leaving you vulnerable to making wrong decisions: quick changes like moving home, remarriage or changing job, etc. This means that each day needs to be treated separately and life in the early stages of bereavement must be lived a day at a time. It helps to know that grief like a wound—a wound of the heart—will need time to heal.

But I would ... that ye sorrow not, even as others which have no hope. (1 Thessalonians 4:13, KJV)

Grief is an intensely powerful experience which leaves one feeling powerless, deprived and hurting and it will take great emotional adjustment to get back to normal. The grief that is awakened by a death can be quite prolonged and you will take some time to recover. It is so powerful at times that 'it tears life to shreds' and may take years to get over. Grief generates shock and often leaves one feeling numb, stunned and so bewildered that it makes it impossible to grasp fully what has happened to you. It is best to trust God at all times, submitting to His providence, while remembering that help and peace will soon come from heaven. Older widows are advised that it may take some years to get over a death and some never really recover or reach normality again. Children will adjust with help from family and friends but patience is necessary.

Anger is another strong emotion connected with death and it is more often than not linked with the questions 'Why?' or 'Why me?' or 'Why now?' This leads to enquiry and seeking answers from medical staff, police, doctors, the clergy and family members. Anger can be directed towards persons or an event and even towards God Himself resulting in a sense of injustice which questions God's providences and love and will tempt one to be bitter (Ruth 1:20–21).

Bitterness brings anger, evil speaking, and malice together (Ephesians 4:31) because it is a rotting bog that will swallow up all kindness and joy (Hebrews 12:15). It will make one retreat from others, rebel against forgiveness and make one redundant in Jesus' divine service. Non-repentance of bitterness will destroy all spiritual life in a professing believer (cf. Mark 6:19). Personal repentance is the antidote for the poison of bitterness (Ephesians 4:32). Bitterness increases our own suffering by injuring the soul and souring the heart. It has to do with holding a resentful spirit that refuses reconciliation. Our fallen human natures often respond with resentment when we are hurt. This can lead to a reservoir of revulsion in the soul that will break fellowship with our Father in heaven and others and result in personal backsliding. Its effects are removal of joy, increase of criticism, a lack of prayer and sustained resentment towards God while the heart remains hardened.

Hope and patience are alive and well only when God's people look forward to the fulfilment of the promise of life after death which is 'the hope of their calling' (Ephesians 1:18). Charles Spurgeon held his hope and said:

The glorified [Christian] weeps no more, for all outward causes of grief are gone. They weep no more, for they are perfectly sanctified. They are without fault before

His throne, because all fear of change is past knowing that they are eternally secure. Sin is shut out, and they are shut in. They drink of a river which shall never dry; they pluck fruit from a tree which shall never wither. They are forever with the Lord and every desire is fulfilled. Eye and ear, heart and hand, judgement, imagination, hope, desire, will, all the faculties, are completely satisfied. We know enough by the revelation of the Spirit, that the saints above are supremely blessed. That same joyful rest remains for us. It may not be far distant. 'Wherefore comfort one another with these words.'[45]

When bereavement and loss strike let Christian hope carry us through as we trust in Christ Jesus for peace and renewed grace in our time in a season of need and sorrow (Hebrews 4:16).

The sick and dying

Divine healing and the desire for miracles when illness strikes are natural to us and we have a varied mix of approaches and understanding throughout Christendom. It is my conviction the Epistle of James chapter 5 gives the best approach and understanding of the pastor's role for requests to pray for the sick.

Is anyone among you suffering? Let him pray. Is anyone cheerful? Let him sing psalms. Is anyone among you sick? Let him call for the elders of the church, and let them pray over him, anointing him with oil in the name of the Lord. And the prayer of faith will save the sick, and the Lord will raise him up. And if he has committed sins, he will be forgiven. (James 5:13–16)

The word that James used for sickness was common but it indicated a serious problem (Greek *asthenos*, i.e. 'without strength'). It is used of Lazarus (John 11:2), so Jesus knew he would die; also Dorcas (Acts 9:37), who was sick and died; Epaphroditus (Philippians 2:27) who was sick

---

45 C.H. Spurgeon, *Morning & Evening*, 23 August (adapted).

'almost unto death' and Trophimus (2 Timothy 4:20) who was left by Paul sick in Miletus (did he die?). These persons were so weak and very seriously ill that prayer was needed on their behalf. These verses lay down what a believer has to do if they have a life-threatening illness and are the clearest and definitive instructions in the New Testament. Notice the procedure commanded:

1. Call the elders of the local church (not a healer of dubious origin). These must be godly men (pl.) who are called into office by the Lord Jesus and His Spirit and recognised by the local churches. Note: some are like Simon Magus who coveted this office and 'power' for himself (Acts 8:18).

2. The initiative is to be with the sick person or their relatives: 'Is anyone among you sick? Let *him* call for the elders of the church.'

3. Meet in the home of the sick person. Let there be no outward show of 'power' to impress before a crowd. Both Elijah and Elisha healed but were shut away alone with the sick person. Peter is also recorded as doing the same in the case of Dorcas—he put them all out (Acts 9:40).

4. Anoint with oil. Is this literal or, as some would prefer, a symbolic action, i.e. with oil on head or on a wound? Is it symbolic of the presence of the Holy Spirit? In other words no actual oil but in the presence and name of Jesus Christ who bestowed the 'oil' of the Spirit by the laying on of hands?

5. However, if called to pray in accordance with James 5, pray over the sick person, anointing with oil as a symbol of the Holy Spirit in obedience to this biblical model without claiming any special powers but with the authority (warrant) of the Word of God as your guide.

Pray in faith in fellowship with the Father, the Son and the Holy Spirit (1 John 5:14).

It is necessary to remember still: that we believe in miracles and God can and does answer prayer for healing. However, remember life is at best short, no matter how long we live, and the Fall into sin in Eden brought physical death to all (Ecclesiastes 3:1–2a). Thus, there is a day of death for all believers as well as for all the lost (2 Timothy 4:19b). For believers death is their 'coronation day' and the day God, by Christ their Saviour, will complete the good work of His grace and favour in them (Philippians 1:6).

Personal guidance

This topic is best preached on from time to time (especially on the Lord's Day when most are gathered, young and old). It is a prerequisite for Christians seeking God's mind and will on their future in or out of the pastorate. My recent advice to friends is seen below.

Dear Friends

Thanks for your letter and your openness on the need to be clear about God's will at this time. I cannot tell you the answer whether to stay or go but I can lay out for you some comments and principles that may be helpful to you at this time. However, God's Word says, 'I will instruct you and teach you in the way you should go; I will guide you with My eye. Do not be like the horse or like the mule, which have no understanding, which must be harnessed with bit and bridle, else they will not come near you' (Psalm 32:8–9). Please lay hold on this promise.

Today you stand at a crossroads. In your pilgrimage and work for Christ Jesus God has been good and gracious and now you need again to look to your heavenly Father for guidance and answered prayer. This means that you need to:

- seek His will
- learn His mind
- be led by the Holy Spirit
- take a step of faith
- trust Him to provide
- ignore all but His will.

The text above (Psalm 32:8–9) is helpful for the principles in guidance:

1. He *promises to instruct* us in His will: 'I will guide you with My eye.'
2. He *expects you to be sensible*: 'Do not be like the horse or like the mule ...'.

Firstly, however, you need also to look to yourselves in order to walk in the Spirit and be safe whether moving or staying. This depends on what your calling is:

- An evangelist?
- A children's worker?
- An evangelist and church planter?
- A full-time pastor?
- A Bible teacher and scholar?

CALLING IS VITAL

Calling and assurance are what keeps men where God wants them. Part-time men are OK, if called as church planters and need to be tent-makers or evangelists, but the pastoral ministry demands full-time labour with the support of a committed (saved) wife. Assured leading is vital and depends on how we are led. Five 'rules are helpful:

1. Seek *biblical* guidance from your daily devotion; do not depend on random texts 'picked out of the air'. This is very important. God will speak if we will listen and pray for guidance.

2. Seek *providential* guidance but do not depend on it. This comes as you recognise open and closed doors (Revelation 3:7). I was once offered the job of a manager in an off-sea construction company and refused it. The door was open, but that was not my calling.

3. Seek *inner peace* which comes as the Spirit witnesses. Are you at peace about the coming changes? This peace is needful bringing with it strength and hope for tomorrow.

4. The need is *not* the call. For everywhere needs the gospel but there are 'horses for courses' and God will place us where we will fit in. The need is everywhere, so do not use that as a proof of God's leading. Yes, Paul was called to come over and help those in Macedonia but that alone is not enough for assurance. As an evangelist this is OK but as a pastor the call needs to be tested and the other leadings added before a decision is made.

5. Are you *both* in agreement and assured? Are both happy and at peace about the possible move with all its changes?

Ultimately only you can know what God wants you to do and knowing it step out in faith and trust Him.

Guidance	Psalm 3:4	Mark 14:38
	Psalm 32:8–9	Luke 11:9
	Psalm 119:27, 34 and 105	John 15:16
	Proverbs 3:5–7	Philippians 4: 9 and
	Proverbs 16:3	2 Timothy 1:13
		Jude 3
		Revelation 3:7

We are much in prayer for you both at this time. The Lord will lead as you weigh up the issues and look to Him for peace and an open door that He has shown.

Proverbs 16:3

Yours in Christ

Pastor Ian

Conclusion

Other areas are within the pastor's counselling scope require care. One I would mention here is the issue of what is wrongly called *'conversion therapy'* (much debated and to be legislated for in early 2020s). I have never been involved in this practice but I have met men who are now 'straight' following personal conversion to Jesus Christ who by His Spirit was the physician that brought personal change and healing. The main issues here for evangelicals is threefold:

Firstly, 'conversion therapy' is wrongly named in a time when biblical moral standards are now rejected by many contemporary non-believers and thus the idea of conversion unto holiness (justification and sanctification) of life is rejected for other non-biblical hypotheses.

Secondly, 'conversion therapy' does not work! We need to recognise that no matter what a second party says (or prays) or does; because God alone changes the human heart so the individual must believe and pray for himself.[46] All and any amount of creature force is useless for, 'A man convinced against his will is of the same opinion still' (as often quoted by others). The gospel is clear: that unless God's free grace in Jesus is known personally and powerfully we *all* remain slaves to our fallen sinful passions and remain lost. Christians teach that it is necessary for the Holy Spirit

---

46 That is not to say the believing prayer is not powerful before God. See my *Getting to grips with prayer* (Leominster: Day One, 2017).

to bring life to a dead soul (John 3:3,7ff). The Arminian's[47] approach to demon-possession and counselling (and that seems to be the source for the great opposition now faced today and not just a simple 'pastor's prayer' during counselling) is founded on their flawed understanding of 'free will' (this is not to deny that Satanic influence is still with us today). We are best to understand human free will as did St Augustine of Hippo: 'The will is free to follow its fallen nature' (or similar words), likewise the reformer John Calvin who states elsewhere: 'So depraved is [our] nature that we can be moved or impelled only to evil.'[48] As a result forceful intimidation does not convert. This is obvious when we take into consideration the numerous testimonies that many (if not all) attempts at this 'conversion' have failed to be effective! So why attempt to ban something that does not work, and why propose to ban something that it is not possible? In Christian theology, anthropology and soteriology the fallen human will is 'free', i.e. free to follow its fallen sinful nature; and so to expose an individual to useless pressure in order to change their lifestyle or feelings is to forget that 'salvation is of the Lord' and that it is free grace alone, through faith alone, in Christ alone that changes the heart and fits for heaven. Protestant reformed Christianity believes that God takes the initiative in salvation because of His love for the elect. In fact, without this divine initiative in grace, we all are powerless and lost. This grace we call 'special' or 'evangelical' as opposed to 'common' grace which is for all of us. God's regenerating grace when known writes His law upon our hearts. It 'does not damage free will, but acts upon it in setting it free and then acts through it when it is freed'.[49]

Thirdly, 'conversion therapy' is an attack on Protestant religion and especially the doctrine of the priesthood of all believers.[50] This is

---

47 **Arminian:** 'a follower of *Arminius* (1560–1609), who denied the Calvinistic doctrine of absolute predestination, as well as that of irresistible grace'. © Chambers Harrap Publishers Ltd: The Chambers Dictionary 2003; The Chambers Thesaurus 2004.

48 https://www.thegospelcoalition.org/article/did-john-calvin-believe-in-free-will/

49 cf R. A. Finlayson, *The Story of Theology*, 1969. p. 32.

50 For a fuller treatment see my book, *Getting to Grips with Prayer: its Reality, Challenges and Potential* (Leominster: Day One, 2017), chapter 5.

a distinctive feature of evangelical life which is rooted in the believer's justification by faith alone and their adoption. This is why the believer's prayers have power with God and cry 'Abba, Father' (Romans 8:15; Galatians 4:6). Roman Catholics deny this doctrine and thus they relegate their laity to a second-class status suggesting they appeal to the Virgin Mary rather than the crucified, risen and ascended Saviour. It is needful, in this assault on Protestant evangelical Christian theology and practice, to note that Roman Catholic religion is not endangered by the [proposed] new law as it utterly rejects the reformation doctrine of the priesthood of all believers and encourages, by using a beaded rosary, to engage in praying not for others but rather for *themselves* personally. The doctrine of the priesthood of all believers taught in the New Testament encourages freedom in prayer, helped by the Holy Spirit, on the basis of the merits of Christ alone:

You also, as living stones, are being built up a spiritual house, a holy priesthood, to offer up spiritual sacrifices acceptable to God through Jesus Christ. (1 Peter 2:5; cf, vv. 9–10)

6. The pastor was wise

'No man can reach the highest degrees of any calling or profession, who does not admire and love it, and give himself to it, day by day.' (J. W. Alexander) [51]

'Antinomianism is to be avoided on the one hand and legalism on the other.' (Erroll Hulse) [52]

'A wise man will hear and increase learning, and a man of understanding will attain wise counsel.' (Proverbs 1:5)

'And moreover, because the Preacher was wise, he still taught the people knowledge; yes, he pondered and sought out and set in order many proverbs. The Preacher sought to find acceptable words; and what was written was upright—words of truth.' (Ecclesiastes 12:9–10)

The pastor's wisdom is to be found from both Testaments; thus he needs to grasp as noted that the 'biblical concept of wisdom is quite different from the classical view that thought philosophy and human rational thought is used to determine the mysteries of existence and the universe. The first principle of biblical wisdom is that people should humble themselves before God in reverence and worship, obedient to His commands. Wisdom is the ability to judge correctly and to follow the best course of action, based on knowledge and understanding.' [53]

---

51 J. W. Alexander, *Thoughts on Preaching* (Edinburgh: The Banner of Truth Trust, 1988), p. 103.
52 Erroll Hulse, 'What is a Pastor?', *Reformation Today*, No. 249, p. 12.
53 Nelson CD_ROM/Dictionary.

Bible wise

'The Preacher was wise' (Ecclesiastes 12:9), i.e. he was wise because of saving grace and was possessed of gifts given to the under-shepherds of God's flock. He is not to be commended as if he is the author of such gifts but he is to see in Christ the source of all spiritual gifts possessed (1 Corinthians 1:24). He recognises that 'the Holy Scriptures are able to make us wise for salvation through faith in Christ Jesus' (2 Timothy 3:15).

The preacher (spoken of in the text above) is to be wise, diligent and careful in his presentation of truth. This calls for a comprehensive and considered approach to the needed disciplines of ministry such as theology, soteriology, ecclesiology, eschatology and history (the last being helpful for context and in search of origin issues and awareness of error and heterodoxy); encouraging, admonishing teaching, counselling and comforting are important tasks for the man of God to perfect. King Solomon, whose source of ideas was from the Shepherd of Israel, set out a wisdom that is not of this world, knowing that: 'wisdom is better than rubies' and 'the wisdom of this world is foolishness with God' (Proverbs 8:11; 1 Corinthians 3:19). It is given to instruct in the art of pastoring and preaching well. 'The Preacher was wise' when he *taught the people knowledge*' (v.9). This task embraces both truth (facts and information) and interpretation aided by the Holy Spirit with the Protestant Christian world-view now extant. Truth that agrees with reality and spoken clearly without spin or bias *'pondered, sought out, set in order'* brings to us the oracles of God to be obeyed (Haggai 1:13). The three verbs describe activity and may also be translated, 'weighed, examined and arranged'[54]. Thus preaching is a high and onerous calling, because 'The Preacher sought to find acceptable words; and what was written was upright—words of truth' (Ecclesiastes 12:13) The conscientious preacher devotes his time to preparing satisfactory words (about the Trinitarian God and His way of salvation) and pleasant words of grace and gospel (for the people

---

54 CD_ROM, Nelson's NKJV Study Bible.

under his care). The Bible is the text book of saving truth and the wisdom of the Christian. Bible commentaries and the confessional statements of Protestantism are their chosen interpreters (surely!). Knowing that 'The Holy Scripture is the only sufficient, certain, and infallible rule of all saving knowledge, faith, and obedience, although the light of nature, and the works of creation and providence do so far manifest the goodness, wisdom, and power of God, as to leave men inexcusable; yet are they not sufficient to give that knowledge of God and His will which is necessary unto salvation'.[55]

Pastors and preachers are to study so as show themselves knowledgeable of God to their peer groups (contemporaries), aiming at edification and spiritual growth while maintaining the church of the living God as 'the pillar and ground of the truth'. Pastors are to be sufficiently knowledgeable so as to encourage their parishioners to attend twice weekly Lord's Day worship. The English Puritan Richard Baxter (1615–1691) was not averse to preaching a difficult sermon on a regular basis, so that his hearers would not become too proud and think themselves wiser than the preacher! He said, 'Be careful that you do not continually feed them only on milk. If they are not fed often with strong meat, they have a tendency to become exceedingly puffed up with pride. If they continually hear nothing from the minister than what they already know, then they think themselves equal to you and as wise as you are.'[56]

In writing to pastor Timothy Paul was insistent: 'Be diligent to present yourself approved to God, a worker who does not need to be ashamed, rightly dividing the word of truth. But shun profane and idle babblings, for they will increase to more ungodliness' (2 Timothy 2:15–16). Rightly dividing is not just breaking up the Bible into dispensations but rather seeing an overview of redemption history from Genesis to Revelation. Young pastors/preachers will learn as they expound the Scriptures and

---

55 Chapter 1: *Of the Holy Scriptures*, para. 1; The London Baptist Confession of Faith 1689.
56 Richard Baxter, *The Reformed Pastor*, p. 98.

preach its themes. The Scriptures are to be taken to heart and pastors need to be ready to acknowledge the divine wisdom, forsaking fallen man's attempts at unbelieving interpretations. Solomon knew that many (human) books are of no use to the servants of God: 'And further, my son, be admonished by these. Of making many books there is no end, and much study is wearisome to the flesh' (Ecclesiastes 12:12). The man of God is to search the Scriptures, serving up wholesome gospel truths. Charles Bridges put it thus: 'The mass of books accumulating is the best comment upon this verse. How many of them are utterly useless! How small a proportion even of what is valuable can be read by one man!' [57] There is no end to the writing and publishing of books, and it is exhausting to try to read them all. Solomon refers to understanding which is his theme in Ecclesiastes because a life if lived without the knowledge of God would be a life lived in vain: for the wisdom of men is not salvation (cf. 12:13–14). Alternatively, he is just simply signifying that the commitment to study and the effort required to ponder and seek out and set in order many proverbs in acceptable and words of truth requires that pastors should not ignore their personal need of a 'sabbath rest' each week to maintain that good mental and physical health necessary for the demands of their calling.

Under-shepherds and overseers

Pastors are God's under-shepherds and overseers. Two texts are pertinent when considering the important topic of pastors in local churches. They both exhort pastors to 'shepherd the flock of God … serving as overseers, 'not by compulsion but willingly, not for dishonest gain but eagerly; nor as being lords over those entrusted to you, but being examples to the flock; and when the Chief Shepherd appears, you will receive the crown of glory that does not fade away' (1 Peter 5: 2–4). They call pastors to be visible examples to be followed in both world-view and lifestyle:

57 Charles Bridges, *Ecclesiastes* (Edinburgh: The Banner of Truth Trust, 1985), p. 308.

'Remember those who rule over you, who have spoken the word of God to you, *whose faith follow*, considering the outcome of their conduct' (Hebrews 13:7).[58] Men of faith and love are required to lead in evangelical churches, as was the case in the early church. Their faith is to be followed, *but not* their mistakes and hang-ups or errors, nor their ambitions which may contradict the Scriptures or bypass church order if procedures are not followed with respect for the members and their opinions. To do so is to lord it over those entrusted to you. Spurgeon was strong on keeping to the Scriptures: 'I have no sympathy with the preaching which degrades the Truth of God into a hobbyhorse for his own thought and only looks upon Scripture as a kind of pulpit which it may thunder out its own opinions.'[59]

Pastors are Christ's under-shepherds and ought to be patient, kind and protective while watching out for each individual's spiritual health. They are always on duty and always caring—who has heard of a shepherd who is off-duty? Theirs is a demanding and a constant ministry. Elders (*presbuteros*) and overseers (*episkopos*) are pastors, being mature office-bearers who walk humbly before God and men having the spiritual gifts as prescribed. They are administrators with spiritual responsibilities to superintend and conscientiously look after what is committed to their care without being dictatorial (Galatians 5:22–26; Philippians 1:1; 1 Timothy 3:1–7; Titus 1:5–9). This high and demanding calling is not to be undertaken for great gain (money or personal kudos) but for love of Christ and His church. The two words for the ruling eldership clarify the point at issue; viz. ruling elders are to be regarded as the same order of government borrowed from the synagogue model. The meaning and usage of *presbuteros* and *episkopos* in the New Testament show that they both apply to the supervising elders (Acts 20:17–18; Titus 1:5–9). The New Testament churches always had more than one elder (*episkopos*) if possible

---

58 Italics mine.
59 C.H. Spurgeon, *The Metropolitan Tabernacle Pulpit*, Vol. 51, 1905, p. 3.

(Acts 14:23). However, the vast majority of early primitive churches would have been small and so we cannot say that *presbyter* technically means *preacher*, but elders are to be 'able to preach' (1 Timothy 3:2).[60] It is necessary also to keep in view the exhortation from Paul when recognising church officers:

Let the elders who rule well be counted worthy of double honour, especially those who labour in the word and doctrine. For the Scripture says, 'You shall not muzzle an ox while it treads out the grain,' and, 'The labourer is worthy of his wages.' (1 Timothy 5:17–18)

Paul here indicates that there is a single elder who is mainly responsible for the regular ministry of the Word of God (following the apostles' example—Acts 6:4). It is clear that pastors are to be examples to their flocks, as church members are exhorted to 'consider the outcome of their conduct' (Hebrews 13:7b). Words are not enough to gain a good character, but obedience to the precepts, piety and holiness sanctified by the Holy Spirit are paramount in the leaders of God's local churches. Faith that clings to Christ at all times is to be publicly demonstrated and pastor/elders are to 'be steadfast, immovable, always abounding in the work of the Lord, knowing that your labour is not in vain in the Lord' (1 Corinthians 15:58) while 'putting their hand to the plough' and keeping on steadfastly in Christ without turning back. Pastors must not browbeat the congregation, nor bind their conscience so that they can be lorded over. The Lord has given to His churches leaders worthy of respect and support. Theirs is a high and holy calling which fools should not envy nor pursue. They are to look after those entrusted to their care with meekness

---

60 Cf Robert L. Dabney (1820–1898), *'Theories of Eldership'*, in David W. Hall & Joseph H. Hall, eds, *Paradigms in Polity: Classic Readings in Reformed and Presbyterian Church Government* (Grand Rapids, MI: Eerdmans Publishing, 1994), pp. 538–557.

so when the Chief Shepherd appears they 'will receive the crown of glory that does not fade away' (1 Peter 5:4 cf. 1 Thessalonians 2:19).

Legalism and salvation

At the last supper meal Jesus said, 'This cup is the new covenant in My blood' (1 Corinthians 11:25), as in Matthew, 'For this is My blood of the new covenant, which is shed for many for the remission of sins' (Matthew 26:28). The old covenant is passed away and is now superseded by a new and better covenant: 'If that first covenant had been faultless, then no place would have been sought for a second ... in that He says, "A new covenant," He has made the first obsolete' (Hebrews 8:7ff). Paul understanding this, says he has a new ministry, and is a 'minister of the new covenant', not now of the Mosaic Law, which he calls 'of the letter', for now his work and witness is 'of the Spirit' (2 Corinthians 3:6). So the days of the Law as a way of salvation are over forever! Paul calls this the gospel, using the phrase, the 'ministry of righteousness' (3:9). Paul has a new ministry: a gospel ministry. He is convinced of the facts, and he has a strong inner conviction that he is to engage in a ministry that will fulfil his Christ-appointed calling. We must not think then that there is any other way of salvation than by free grace alone. The Holy Spirit must make known the truth through preaching and the gift of transforming grace. These combine to bring repentance, faith and trust in the gospel message. Sinners are to respond well to the gospel call to repentance and believe in the person and work of Jesus Christ and His resurrection from the dead on the third day (1 Corinthians 15:1–4ff).

Is the Law still relevant now? In 2 Corinthians 3:6 Paul says he is a servant of the new covenant (Greek = *diatheke*). So is the old still operative? In this portion of Scripture Paul contrasts the old and new covenants by saying the old was glorious but the new is greater, 'For even what was made glorious had no glory in this respect, because of the glory that excels. For if what is passing away was glorious, what remains is much more glorious' (2 Corinthians 3:10–11).

Legalism is a term bandied about a lot in evangelical circles but often used in a wrong way. It properly means the use of law *as a way of salvation*. We know as Protestants that that is a serious error. To endeavour to get to heaven by personal good works and participation in the sacraments rather than looking to the blood of Christ alone for atonement and forgiveness denies the gospel of free grace. This is heresy and a denial of justification by faith alone.

The cry of legalism is used wrongly when it accuses sincere believers of trying to live lives which respect the Ten Commandments, and thus is a wrong use of the term. Legalism applies not to discipleship but to Pharisaism—a way of procuring salvation by rule-keeping—while obedience (as well as faith) is about ongoing sanctification. When defining 'legalism' it is good to remember that if the Law is used in order to justify the sinner, that is legalism (Romans 5:1; Hebrews 11:6). If the Law is used as a covenant of works to gain salvation, that is also legalism (Colossians 2:16–17). It is clear, however, that the Law was and is intended as a schoolmaster to bring the sinner to repentance and to faith in Christ (Galatians 3:24). Legalism is what the *cults* practise and what the 'cultish' churches and assemblies use to control their membership.

The correct definition of legalism is crucial to understanding the way of salvation. Get it wrong and all sorts of problems remain for sincere worshippers and unsaved sinners. It is clear that the Law was and is intended to bring the sinner to repentance and to faith in Christ.

But before faith came, we were kept under guard by the law, kept for the faith which would afterward be revealed. Therefore the law was our tutor to bring us to Christ, that we might be justified by faith. But after faith has come, we are no longer under a tutor [as a way of salvation]. (Galatians 3:23–25)

Legalistic 'righteousness' cannot save, as salvation is by faith alone, in Christ alone that imputes (reckons) righteousness to the sinner, that is the gospel (Romans 3:21–26). A personally created holiness is not what the gospel is all about. Salvation is about the Law written on the heart (Jeremiah 31:33) and thus lived out by faith and love in Jesus Christ:

> For they being ignorant of God's righteousness, and seeking to establish their own righteousness, have not submitted to the righteousness of God. For Christ is the end of the law for righteousness to everyone who believes. (Romans 10:3–4)

Works of self-righteousness and law-keeping (even 613 of them!) will not and do not save us; thus Paul's words: 'Therefore, since we have this ministry, as we have received mercy, we do not lose heart' (2 Corinthians 4:1).

Three categories of law

These can be discerned in the Old Testament, viz., *ceremonial, civil [judicial]* and *moral.*[61] It is traditional to speak of the unity of the Ten Commandments as they hold together as one. The Epistle of James reminds us of this: 'For whoever shall keep the whole law, and yet stumble in one point, he is guilty of all' (James 2:10). God's **moral laws** are meant to be obeyed by all peoples in all generations because they reflect God's character and reveal His will for all mankind.[62] It is therefore wrong to dismiss the fourth commandment as obsolete under the New Covenant. The Baptist Confession of Faith 1689, chapter 19, also lays the three before us.

---

61 J. F. Bayes, *The Threefold division of the law* (Newcastle upon Tyne: The Christian Institute, 2005). See also the *Westminster Confession of Faith*, chapter 19.

62 In Reformed Christian ethics, the creation ordinances include marriage [one man to one woman], procreation (Genesis 1:28), the work mandate (Genesis 2:15), and the one day in seven Sabbath (Genesis 2:3).

Because salvation is by grace alone through Christ alone those saved are not under law as a covenant of works but the Law (Ten Commandments) is applicable to the people of God being a spiritual and holy statement about God. In the Baptist Confession of Faith 1689, chapter 19, 'Of the Law of God', and para. 6, we have four benefits of Law:[63]

1. It brings the knowledge of God's character and will to our attention.

2. It teaches sinners their fallen corruption and destiny. John Wesley said, 'Preach the law before the gospel' (but today this brings evangelicals into culture wars and heavy opposition with the LGBT+ unbelievers).

3. It restrains indwelling sins in the righteous.

4. It opens up the promised blessings by active obedience and abiding.

Antinomianism

Antinomianism is used, 'to describe the rejection of the moral law as a relevant part of the Christian experience'.[64] There are two forms: Peter Toon in his book on Hyper-Calvinism, says doctrinal antinomianism is to be distinguished from practical antinomianism—which abuses God's grace.[65] This distinction is astute since for many their doctrine is very different from their practice while for others doctrine and practice are very closely intertwined. The word *antinomianism* (*anti*, 'against'; *nomos*, 'law') is said first to have been used by Luther in his controversy with his colleague Johannes Agricola. John Calvin (in his *Institutes of Religion*)

---

63 See also the *Westminster Confession of Faith*, chapter 19.
64 Hugh J. Blair, *The New International Dictionary of the Christian Church* (Grand Rapids, MI), p. 48.
65 Peter Toon, *The Emergence of Hyper-Calvinism in English Nonconformity 1689–1765* (London, 1967), p. 28.

wrote against antinomianism by positing three uses of the moral law.[66] So Calvin when he specifically speaks against antinomianism says, 'Some skilful persons ... discard the whole Law of Moses, and do away with both tables, imagining it unchristian to adhere to a doctrine which contains the ministration of death. Far from our thoughts be this profane notion.' He maintains that the law 'ought to have a better and more excellent effect on the righteous' for it contains, 'a perfect pattern of righteousness' and 'rule of life'.[67] He concludes this section on antinomianism by saying, 'The law has lost none of its authority, but must always receive from us the same respect and obedience.'[68]

In the British & Foreign Evangelical Review (B&FER) article on 'Antinomianism' we are reminded that, 'Antinomians have large ideas of Christian liberty, low ideas of sin, and disparaging views of the law.' It clearly shows that antinomianism has thrown overboard the moral law as an authoritative guide and rule of life for believers. Although some brethren would deny this, it does lend itself to that reality: 'They refuse to see in the Bible any positive laws binding on Christians, and regard themselves as left to the guidance of gospel principles, and constraint of Christian love.'[69] The B&FER article reduces antinomianism to three classes:

- *Firstly,* those who believe that the Christian can live as they please without 'prejudice to their sanctity'.

---

66 It is interesting to note that in the *Formula of Concord*, written seventeen years after the definitive edition of Calvin's *Institutes* had appeared (1559), the same three uses of the law are enumerated (although in a slightly different order). In general, the Lutheran theologians characterised the three uses of the Moral Law as 'political,' 'pedagogical,' and 'didactic'. These three uses were expressed in the German terms 'Sundenriegel,' 'Sundenspiegel,' and 'Lebensregel,' which respectively mean 'a restraint against sin,' 'a mirror of sin,' and 'a rule of life'. Cf Calvin's *Institutes*, II: vii, p.810, n.3.
67 Ibid., II:vii:13.
68 Ibid., II:vii:15.
69 *British & Foreign Evangelical Review*, 'Antinomianism', p.26.

- *Secondly,* some hold the moral law has been abrogated and none are subject to its authority (i.e. Ten Commandments).

- *Thirdly,* there are those who 'refuse to see in the Bible any positive laws binding on Christians'.

When this last theory is pushed to its logical limit their doctrine brings believers into a state of *sinless perfection.* So they are against the moral law of God. Hyper-Calvinism has a tendency to antinomianism. Libertines and false Christians are prone to this grave error.

What are we saying?

If the professing pastor or a believer lives as the unsaved do then they cannot complain that they are regarded as unsaved by Christians and also by the world. The Saviour made this plain when He said, 'By their fruits you will know them' (Matthew 7:16–20). A. A. Hodge concurred: 'You cannot take Christ for justification, unless you take Him for sanctification.'[70] To deny a moral righteous witness to the new birth is antinomian. J. I. Packer taught that antinomianism (ideas) 'must be answered in terms, not of justification, but of adoption: a reality which the Puritans never highlighted enough. Justification frees one for ever from the need to keep the law, or try to, as the means of earning life; it is equally true that adoption lays on one the binding obligation to keep the law, as a means of pleasing one's new found Father'.[71]

---

70 A. A. Hodge, *Evangelical theology* (Edinburgh: The Banner of Truth Trust, 1976), p. 310.
71 J. I. Packer, *Knowing God*, pp. 249–250.

7. Pastor and people (1)

'Another part of our ministerial oversight consists in the right
comforting of the conscience of those who are troubled.
We must settle our people in a well grounded peace.'
(Richard Baxter)[72]

*'The God and Father of our Lord Jesus Christ, the Father of mercies and
God of all comfort, who comforts us in all our tribulation, that we may be
able to comfort those who are in any trouble, with the comfort with which
we ourselves are comforted by God.'* (2 Corinthians 1:3–4)

'To Philemon our beloved friend and fellow labourer.' (Philemon 1b)

The small Epistle to Philemon was written by the apostle Paul
(v. 1). There is a close relationship between the Epistle to
Philemon and the Epistle to the Colossians, firstly because the
church in Colosse met in Philemon's house (vv. 1–2) and secondly because
both epistles were written about the same time when Paul was imprisoned
in Rome. It was written to secure forgiveness and freedom for the slave
Onesimus, to strike at the heart of slavery, and to request a place of
lodging for Paul after his release (v. 22). It was sent from Rome around
AD 60–62. There is only one chapter in this small epistle; however, it
can instruct pastors on how to get their people to do what is right in
God's eyes.

---

72 Richard Baxter, *The Reformed Pastor*, p. 20.

Paul's calling

Paul is a 'prisoner' in the service of Christ and for the sake of Christ he makes this clear in v. 1. When he writes this letter he is imprisoned in Rome because of his commitment to Christ Jesus and His church and shows willingness to suffer. Paul was willing to give up his rights for the gospel and his Saviour's glory. When Paul wrote the words, 'Paul ... a prisoner of Christ Jesus' (v. 1) he did not consider himself a prisoner of the Roman Empire but of the King of kings, the Lord Jesus Christ Himself. So his situation (this providence) was all in the plan of Christ as far as Paul was concerned. This he acknowledges when he calls himself *a prisoner of Christ Jesus.* This confinement meant that practically he was under fiscal restraint which severely restricted his personal freedom to do as he pleased. It also meant metaphorically he was a prisoner of Christ's; he could not be free of God's will even if he wanted to be! Paul became a prisoner to Christ's love when on the road to Damascus where it found him and called him to repentance and faith. It had captivated and enslaved him since the day of his conversion (Ephesians 4:1).

Three things can be noted regarding Paul as *a prisoner of the Lord:*

(i) While in prison Paul *redeemed the time.* He wrote the 'prison epistles'; viz. the epistles to the Ephesians, Philippians, Colossians and Philemon (cf. Colossians 4:4; Ephesians 5:16). The church owes a great debt to God for arranging this so that it could have these letters. What Paul might have been tempted to describe as 'negative providences against him' was in fact positive planning by God for the good of the churches in Christendom (Colossians 1:24). While confined he *redeemed the time* by witnessing to those around him (perhaps this was how Onesimus came to hear the gospel and believe in Christ?). Another use of his time in captivity is seen in his prayer life for the saints which was strong and energetic (Ephesians 3:14ff; Philippians 1:9–11; Colossians 1:9ff). Paul believed that prayer is effectual with God and so he prayed much while he had the opportunity in prison (v. 22; 2 Corinthians 1:11). There are

times in ministry when pastors feel they can't get free of *their* situation. Their time must not be wasted; keep praying for yourself and the church knowing that God can change things, and say with the psalmist, 'My soul, wait silently for God alone, for my expectation is from Him' (Psalm 62:5 cf. Romans 12:12).

(ii) While providentially hindered he was content with the Lord's plans for his life and ministry. We see this from Philippians 4:11–12, 'I have learned in whatever state I am, to be content: I know how to be abased, and I know how to abound' (cf. also v. 19).

(iii) In ministry Paul was willing to take up his cross daily, and be led by the Holy Spirit and providence. As a servant of Jehovah, Paul did not lose faith in Christ or his love for the saints because of his problems. He continued to do what was right and holy irrespective of his circumstances. He put aside any bitterness and his difficulties for Christ's sake. He kept the faith and stayed in love with his Saviour (cf.Philemon 5). Pastors are called to put their hands to the plough and not turn back.

Paul was a 'prisoner' called to journey along the 'Narrow Way that leads to life'. At points in our journey we may stray into *By-pass Meadow* and there be caught by a terrible creature called *Giant Despair* and thrown into *Doubting Castle* to experience depression and fear and become a prisoner not of the God of love but of the doubts of Giant Unbelief. In John Bunyan's allegory (*The Pilgrim's Progress*) the two pilgrims are beaten many times by the giant until in their misery they seek the Lord in believing prayer. Bunyan wrote: 'On Saturday about midnight, they began to pray and continued in prayer until almost break of day.' Only then did the two companions realise that the key to the dungeon door of Doubting Castle was with them all along. The key to the door was faith in the promises of God. When they remembered the promises and believed them afresh the key made the door fly open and they ran for their lives out and through the meadow and over the fence back onto the *Narrow Way that leads to life*. Now free, they went on their way to the Celestial City rejoicing once again. In this allegory these two believers ended up in a prison and it was their own fault! Pastors are to be patient on the Narrow Way that leads to life, for it runs at times through stony ground and up steep hills and across deep rivers. Remember that John Bunyan was himself in prison for twelve years because he would not stop preaching the gospel. To make it to heaven we must exercise faith and patience and be shod with the shoes of the gospel of peace: 'My brethren, be strong in the Lord and in the power of His might. Put on the whole armour of God, that you may be able to stand against the wiles of the devil' (Ephesians 6:10–11).

At the outset of his short letter Paul acknowledges Philemon's friendship and work (vv. 1b–2) and sends warm greetings to his wife and the church through him. This bond led to a commitment to pray for Philemon personally and for his fruitful ministry of preaching and teaching. There is also reassurance in Paul's praise for Philemon which surely was well received: 'We have great joy and consolation in your love, because the hearts of the saints have been refreshed by you, brother' (v. 7). This quality of relationship is to be encouraged and Paul's care to give praise where praise is due is to be noted.[73] Paul, however, omits to say in his introduction that he is an apostle as he did in his letter to the Colossians (and as he does in earlier Epistles). Why was this? It appears that he is 'walking softly' and moving slowly to make a request in a respectful and careful manner.

Paul's examples

(i) HIS ATTITUDE

The request from Paul to Philemon is an appeal for the freedom of the slave Onesimus. Paul could have been bossy and ordered him to obey, but he was polite and gracious (Paul's right to rule as an apostle is taught in the Scriptures (Romans 1:1; 1 Corinthians 5:3–4; 9:1; Galatians 1:1;

---

73 This is to be preferred to the attitude of some church members not to praise or encourage in case their pastor get a 'big head'!

2 Corinthians 10:13–14; 12:12). In verse 8 Paul acknowledges his authority to order Philemon to obey; however, he holds back: 'I might be very bold in Christ to command you what is fitting, yet for love's sake I rather appeal to you.' For members of independent churches who are used to living with the doctrine of the priesthood of all believers the concept of someone having authority over them in religious matters is often unacceptable even when he is Christ Jesus' under-shepherd: 'Oh no, we don't want that!' However, Paul knowing human nature and out of love for Philemon speaks gently to him because he wants him to respond in love to both himself and the slave. Pastors are to do the same when seeking co-operation and support. They will rarely get their people to do what *God* wants using intimidating or overbearing tactics; there is a more biblical way—a better way. Paul is gentle and patient in spirit using a 'man management' technique as an example to us all. He fully respects his friendship with Philemon and because of this his words are supportive (vv. 4–7), informative (vv.8–16) and courteous (vv.17–21). Paul is on Philemon's side and he lets him know it. This being said, there is a better attitude now expected and Paul wants Philemon to do the right thing and to free the redeemed slave. Paul aims, through his request, to convince Philemon that he should receive his returning slave with mercy and joy. Onesimus is now a brother beloved in Christ and should be acknowledged as such and therefore given his freedom. Would Philemon agree to do this?

There is something remarkable here. This Jewish scholar, this Pharisee of the Pharisee, accepted a Gentile slave as his brother! Oh, how God's free grace changes people's attitude as well as their destiny (Colossians 3:11; Ephesians 2:14)! Christians are to accept those whom Christ accepts. Consider 1 Corinthians 1:26–31, 'For you see your calling, brethren, that not many wise according to the flesh, not many mighty, not many noble, are called. But God has chosen the foolish things of the world to put to shame the wise, and God has chosen the weak things of the world to put to shame the things which are mighty ...'. Paul knows all about this saving grace first-hand as he had been received as a bona fide believer by the apostles and James the Lord's brother, although he was previously a persecutor of Christians before his conversion (Acts 9:26; Galatians 1:18–19; cf. Luke 15:11–32). How wonderful to see in all this the power of the gospel and its ability to remove prejudice and bigotry from the heart!

(ii) HIS APPEAL

It is clear that Paul petitions Philemon on the basis of Christian love: 'I appeal to you for my son Onesimus, whom I have begotten while in my chains, who once was unprofitable to you, but now is profitable to you and to me' (v. 10). This is an example of Paul's pastoral care and respect. The mind of Christ was in Paul (Philippians 2:5) as we note, when writing to the Corinthians, Paul appealed to the church there in the 'meekness and gentleness of Christ' (2 Corinthians 10:1). The gentle spirit of love is the strongest of all requests (1 Corinthians 16:14). Paul had *three grounds* of appeal:

Firstly, he is an apostle.

Secondly, he is a prisoner who is willing to suffer for his Saviour's sake (was Philemon willing to give up his rights for Christ's sake and free Onesimus?).

Thirdly, Paul is Onesimus' spiritual father in the Lord and beloved in Christ.

There was also a fourth reason why Philemon should listen to Paul: yes, Onesimus was not guiltless, nevertheless God used his rebellion to bring about his salvation. Thus Onesimus' outlook and attitudes are now sanctified in Christ Jesus to the extent that he was willing to go back to his master and 'face the music'. Conversion changes people permanently. Onesimus was willing to do what was right and trust the Lord. People are only *profitable* (useful) when they are good servants of Christ (Matthew 25:14–30). By Onesimus' willingness to return we see true repentance. He was willing to admit his crime and pay for it if necessary (cf. 2 Corinthians 7:9ff).

(iii) HIS ANTICIPATION

Paul is so attached to Onesimus that it feels as if he is losing part of himself (vv. 12–13) by his returning home: 'I am sending him back. You therefore receive him, that is, my own heart, whom I wished to keep with me … But without your consent I wanted to do nothing, that your good deed might not be by compulsion, as it were, but voluntary' (vv. 12–14). The expression *my own heart* is the same as in v.7 and speaks of the affections and emotions Paul is experiencing as he writes. This sincere Gentile believer was redeemed. The apostle will not coerce his friend but hopes that grace will triumph in his heart and he will do as requested (2 Timothy 2:24–25a).

Conclusion

There are some things that must be left to the believer's own conscience. These we call 'secondary' matters. They are not unimportant and they must be discerned from the pages of Scripture and agreed by each church. There are other things that are necessary to the unity and peace of the local churches, especially the exercise of patience and love. Also important to individual Protestant denominations, independent local churches whether congregational or Baptist etc., are their Articles of Faith and Unity. However, freedom of individual conscience is not for sale nor is it to be mistreated. When it comes to the individual saints their renewed conscience is a powerful tool in the hands of the Holy Spirit. Everyone is free to let their conscience speak, but they must make sure that it is guided by the Scriptures and the Holy Spirit of God. We read in verse 14b 'that your good deed might not be by compulsion, as it were, but voluntary', i.e. not forced. The Greek is *agathon*, which speaks of what is (intrinsically) good. Will Philemon's 'good' (or goodness) be out of love from his heart and not just a cold or calculating obedience? Calvin is right to say: 'Only freely offered sacrifices are pleasing to God,' and the Bible says 'God loves a cheerful giver' (2 Corinthians 9:7). Freedom of conscience is a recognised part of Protestant religious freedom. People must not be press-ganged into conforming to their pastor's wishes. Everything is not black or white. The pastor's good (or goodness) must be out of love and not just from an administrative zeal. 'Love suffers long and is kind … bears all things … endures all things. Love never fails.' Paul is not dogmatic here and he puts his request graciously: 'For perhaps he departed for a while for this purpose, that you might receive him forever, no longer as a slave but more than a slave—a beloved brother' (vv. 15–16). This request does not contradict the doctrine of providence. Onesimus' departure from Colosse was deliberate on his own part but God meant it for good (cf. Genesis 45:5; Romans 8:28). Providence has to do with God's sovereign planning and overruling. There are real mysteries in the providences of God. Paul is not ashamed to call Onesimus *a beloved brother*, so Philemon should do so too. Onesimus is to be considered now as a brother, forgiven as a brother, received as a brother and treated like a brother beloved: 'especially to me but how much more to you, both in the flesh and in the Lord'.

Pastors need to possess big helpings of diplomacy. This is demonstrated by Paul's offer to pay reparation. It is very probable that Onesimus owed money to Philemon and that is what is introduced here. If there is debt there must be reconciliation and restitution between master and slave or Paul's plan would fail. Thus Paul is willing to 'put his money where his mouth is' and promises that if it is necessary he will pay Onesimus' debt: 'If he has wronged you or owes anything, put that on my account' (v. 18). Paul authenticates his offer by signing this promise: 'I, Paul, am writing with my own hand. I will repay.' The reality was that Philemon owed Paul a greater debt: 'You owe me even your own self besides' (v. 19). Philemon was renowned for a ministry of refreshing (v. 7). This Greek verb, *anapauō*, has the idea of 'rest' and 'restoration', therefore 'to refresh', and thus it appears that Paul anticipates compliance over Onesimus' future, 'Having confidence in your obedience, I write to you, knowing that you will do even more than I say' (v. 21).

William Hendriksen in his commentary calls this epistle a 'Masterpiece of Tactful Pleading' and defines tactfulness 'as a virtue which is the product of special grace. Its parents are love and wisdom and its children are humility, patience and kindness'.[74] Paul as a skilled pastor aims to maintain fellowship and trust in his relationship with Philemon. He also hopes to see Philemon again if his prayers and corresponding requests are positively answered and fellowship with his brother in the Lord continues (v. 22). Pastors are to pray that they will possess tact and patience in their calling to shepherding of the little flock of God, in order to keep the unity of the Spirit in the bond of peace (Ephesians 4:3).

---

74 W. Hendriksen, *Colossians and Philemon* (London: The Banner of Truth Trust, 1971), p. 226.

8. Pastor and people (2)

'A pastor is different from the ruling elders of the local church because he is to give himself wholly to the ministry. In that complete commitment he must dedicate himself to acquiring the skills necessary for the full-time ministry.' (Erroll Hulse) [75]

'Walk worthy of the calling with which you were called, with all lowliness and gentleness, with longsuffering, bearing [anechomenoi] with one another in love, endeavouring to keep the unity of the Spirit in the bond of peace.' (Ephesians 4:1–3)

'Be kind one to another, tenderhearted, forgiving one another, even as God in Christ forgave you.' (Ephesians 4:32)

Why is the pastor like a boxer? Because he is left alone in the 'ring' fighting the spiritual battle for the whole church! As he does so it feels as if the congregation is looking on and shouting advice for him to do well. In the course of the bout he takes all the punishment and all the beating and by the end he is exhausted and needs rest. This is, of course, the wrong illustration of good and well-organised local church life. However, it can happen and the pastor can feel alone and unsupported by his leadership team and members. It is better for him and the leaders to be like a tug-of-war team with every person on hand and engaged. Or perhaps a better illustration is for the church to emulate a football team with each player having a job to do using his talents and supporting the game plan. This is what Paul speaks of in First Corinthians:

---

75 Erroll Hulse, 'What is a Pastor?', *Reformation Today*, No. 249, p. 11.

For as the body is one and has many members, but all the members of that one body, being many, are one body, so also is Christ. For by one Spirit we were all baptized into one body—whether Jews or Greeks, whether slaves or free—and have all been made to drink into one Spirit. For in fact the body is not one member but many. (12:12–14)

The local churches are called to reach out to their community and locality bearing witness to the love and grace of Christ their Saviour with the fruits of the new birth and practice. Disunity in local churches resulting in secessions or splits will linger for a long time in the memory of the local population and thus hinder the local witness and the effectiveness of evangelism and good works (Ephesians 4:1–6, 30–32). Church members' meetings are in the main run as dictated by the church rules/constitution or whatever document is extant for this purpose. It is proper that the rules are followed so as the leaders as well as the members are sure of established procedures. The rule books (Constitutions and Trust Deeds) are best followed to give sound, proper and official guidance at meetings. There are times when the temptation is to ignore or rewrite procedures; however, this is to be avoided as it can smell of dictatorship, hubris and disrespect for the local church. No rule books can hold all the answers to problems that may arise in church life; nonetheless, a good and Bible-based 'Church Rules' will in the main give a lead on how to handle issues that arise. Pastors must resist the temptation in times of conflict with leaders or members to ignore or overturn the agreed constitution. If the rules need changing then the church members need to be involved before amendments are made. Difficult church meetings can be a real test of the pastor's gifts and the leaders' graces while the members bear and forbear as its leaders suggest changes or projects. The members are to be allowed to speak (in proper order and as led from the front by a chairman) and to be given respect, and their freedom acknowledged in the church rules. The members need time and explanation before votes are taken according to the rules and room has to be given for alternative proposals duly seconded.

Dealing with differences

There is a tendency to overreact and to exercise too much or too little discipline. In all cases it is pertinent to remember that the apostle clarifies what he regards as a correct attitude: 'Do not count him as an enemy, but admonish him as a brother' (2 Thessalonians 3:15). 'Admonition' is a strong word (*noutheteō*) and means 'to put in mind' (Ephesians 6:4). To quote R. C. Trench, 'It is the training by word—by the word of encouragement, when this is sufficient, but also by that of remonstrance, of reproof, of blame, where these may be required.'[76] All church discipline is intended to restore and reinstate the fallen and is not designed to punish (that is the prerogative of God; cf. Romans 12:19–21). The end in view is the return of the backslidden or fallen believer to spiritual health and into full fellowship within the local church. All discipline must be undertaken in the spirit of love and humility with the best motives and the glory of Christ in view (Galatians 6:1–2). Conflict is to be handled as the Scriptures teach (Matthew 18:15–17; John 13:34–35; 1 Corinthians 16:11; 1 Peter 4:8).

Local church unity[77]

The unity of the local church can be disrupted in many ways. When writing to the Philippian church Paul had occasion to exhort two lady believers to 'be of the same mind in the Lord' (Philippians 4:2). Their names were Euodia and Syntyche. It seems that they had fallen out over some matter and this was affecting their personal friendship and the church's unity. Here we see the problem of estranged believers. This is not new to 21st century local churches though I suspect it is a persistent problem still in many today. How the work of God is hindered because believers don't get on together! What was the matter in question? It seems from the context (which is about service in the local church) that the disagreement

---

76 R. C. Trench, *Synonyms of the New Testament* (Grand Rapids, MI: W. B. Eerdmans Publishing, 1976), p. 112.

77 From the FIEC Magazine, *Dealing with Differences* (FIEC) 'Fellowship Magazine', Sept/Oct. Vol. 10, No. 5, 1988; by Ian McNaughton; adapted.

was related to church work and no doubt work in which they were both involved. Both were members of the local church, this is clear from verse 3 where Paul writes, 'Help these women who laboured with me in the gospel'. Paul used a Greek verb here which means 'to strive at the same time with another'. Thus they shared Paul's struggle and contended at his side in the cause of Christ together. So they had worked, no doubt, enthusiastically and well together with the great apostle and at that time harmoniously. But alas, dissension arose between those fine women and as a result the progress of the gospel was retarded and the congregation grieved. Euodia and Syntyche are likely to have been influential women. All believers are under obligation to Christ to 'keep the unity of the Spirit in the bond of peace' (Ephesians 4:3). This however, is more necessary for those who are in positions of influence, or are placed to affect others by their attitudes. Most damage can be done by the influential individuals of a congregation. When quarrels arise between such persons, factions often form within the congregation, rallying to either side, and much damage can then result to the local fellowship within and its reputation without. When Paul wrote, 'Let nothing be done through selfish ambition or conceit, but in lowliness of mind let each esteem others better than himself' (2:3) was he thinking of Euodias and Syntyche?

Well-being

It seems obvious from these verses that the disharmony between those one-time friends was known throughout all the fellowship or Paul would not have felt free to make mention of it; so it was public knowledge. It was also an unresolved problem or Paul would have had no reason to raise the matter. What is more, the situation was prolonged. It took time for Paul to hear news from Philippi as he was a prisoner in Rome. Having heard it and being burdened about it he made mention of it in his letter to the church there. So the evidence speaks of a prolonged disharmony. How long? One year, two years? We do not know. This however is certain, it was too long. It also seems there were no black and white issues involved here. I agree with F. B. Meyer who says, 'They were of different dispositions and could not understand each other.' How often this occurs within the church life and only love and patience can overcome this type of thing. Paul does not say one or other is to be blamed. It is obvious that he holds them both in high regard. This is seen simply by the fact that he mentions them at all and by the language he uses. Notice that he does not simply say, 'I beseech Euodia and Syntyche' but he takes each separately and personally in his exhortation (v. 2). He does not point the finger making one out as guilty and the other innocent. No, he treats them both in the same way. If one only was to blame he would have exhorted repentance and possibly discipline and would have made this clear to the church at Philippi. Paul however does not treat this problem as a disciplinary matter. What we have here may be difference in emphasis, approach or attitude. Might it even have been differences related to secondary issues? It is, however, a problem of estrangement and one that is affecting the life and witness of the church at Philippi. These women were Christians—verse 3 makes that clear. There Paul says that their 'names are in the book of life'. His knowledge of their love for Christ and zeal for His gospel convinced him that they belonged to God. 'They were doubtless professing Christians and the Apostle exhorts them to make "the Lord" the great object of their affections and in their regard for Him to bury all their petty differences and animosities' (Albert Barnes, commentary). Paul does not want them to agree about everything in life or in the local church but to agree 'in the Lord'. Pastors too are to guard the harmony, unity and testimony, on their charges as well as their personal relationship. He is to recognise that God takes people from different social backgrounds with different temperaments and with different intellects, saves them and unites them by love to be one Body. How unique, how miraculous! This is God's design for His people and for the local churches.

Chapter 8

Regarding the non-members

Pastors need to recognise that there will be both saved and unsaved in their weekly congregations and also among the members. There will be times when a church officer is not a born again Christian. If so this has to be dealt with as he is able to raise issues in the assembly that are schismatic. In our evangelical churches this is more common than might be expected! When being interviewed by the local church leaders in a vacancy I tried to ascertain their spirituality by asking each one to tell me about his own conversion.

What of those who do not join as members but are regular weekly attendees? Some will have been hurt or distressed by previous spells in church membership; a few will not accept that local church membership is biblical; others will hesitate because of leadership personalities and/or over doctrinal issues. These reasons and others are not uncommon and need to be treated sympathetically with patience, remembering that local church membership is a voluntary issue (although clearly taught in the New Testament). These friends are to be accepted as friends, if in good standing, and as brothers and sisters in the Lord. Good pastoral help may, at length, encourage them to join.

The use of modern technology—the internet like Facebook or WhatsApp—can be problematic if non-members are linked in and thus informed in ways that regular and long-standing members are not (i.e. those not using the apps). This has the potential to cause schism and feelings of isolation with spiritual consequences (the little 'foxes' spoil the vine). The pastor and elders need to be on guard for consequences.

9. What to preach (1)

'The holiest men in the Christian church have been the most studious men.' (W. G. T. Shedd) [78]

'If our preaching is always expository and for edification and teaching it will produce members who are hard and cold, and often harsh and self-satisfied.' (D. Martyn Lloyd-Jones) [79]

'Be careful that you do not continually feed them with only milk. If they are not fed often with stronger meat, they have a tendency to become exceedingly puffed up with pride.' (Richard Baxter) [80]

'... *rightly dividing the word of truth.*' *(2 Timothy 2:15)*

How are preachers and pastors to understand the Word of God? How are they to preach it? It requires the diligence of a scholar and the heart of an evangelist to preach well. God expects those who preach and teach to study in order to understand what the Bible is and what it says. To fail to do this is to forfeit the great privilege of being God's spokesman before God's people. The phrase, '*rightly dividing the word of truth*', has been used to circulate views of Scripture that are spurious and lacking an understanding of the plan of salvation and that fail to assist the presentation of the gospel.

---

78 W. G. T. Shedd, *Homiletics and Pastoral Theology*, p. 286.
79 D. M. Lloyd-Jones, *Preaching and Preachers*, p. 153.
80 Richard Baxter, *The Reformed Pastor*, p. 98.

Protestant theology is best represented and laid out in the post-Reformation confessions. Pastors are to preach a world-view and way of salvation that embraces all of God's Word as inerrant and complete. What is taught about the Scriptures must embrace Jesus Christ's words, 'Your word is truth' (John 17:17) and Paul's statement about the 'house of God, which is the church of the living God, the pillar and ground of the truth' (1 Timothy 3:15). The Bible promotes Jesus Christ as the only Mediator between God and men. There is no priest or prophet greater than Jesus Christ. He died on the cross to save us from our sins, providing eternal life which is freely offered in the gospel. Jesus Christ spoke the words of God which regulates the church's faith and practice. He rose from the dead on the third day to declare that He is the Son of God and the Saviour of the whole world (John 14:6; Acts 4:12; Hebrews 1:2). Allied with this evangelical view is the necessity of experimental religion in the soul, i.e. the new birth. This is a shared mantra among believers. It comes from the Gospel of John chapter 3. Jesus said to the scholar Nicodemus: 'You must be born again.' This subjective work of the Holy Spirit is so overpowering and so life-changing that all evangelicals lay claim to the experience. It is not an optional extra but the beginning of all saving work in the soul which brings with it an assurance that the Bible is true. To reject the Bible as unreliable leaves one with philosophical questions about human consciousness, the origin of life and intelligence and other of man's greatest questions unanswered. Christians are faced with a choice of either accepting the mind of God or the mind of fallen men; the choice is between revealed religion and independent human enquiry. Evangelical Christians believe the Bible is wholly true and is what God wants us to hear, believe and follow. J.I. Packer put it this way: 'Belief that God says what the Scriptures say is in truth the foundation-stone of all New Testament theology'[81] (cf. Titus 1:2). It is essential that important topics are taught in a pulpit ministry. These are:

---

81 J.I. Packer, *God Has Spoken: Revelation and the Bible* (London: Hodder & Stoughton, 1985), pp. 23, 24.

The inerrancy of the Bible

How are we to see God's good book? I answer: through eyes enlightened by the Holy Spirit. Protestant evangelicals believe in the infallibility of the Bible and in a God-given and protected Bible. It is one Holy Book written over a period of 1,600 years by about 40 authors and contains 66 books (39 Old Testament and 27 New Testament) written in Hebrew, Aramaic and koine Greek. These authors and books are in complete harmony as to the nature of God, the pre- and post-incarnation nature of Jesus Christ and the doctrine of man created in God's image (this makes it unique among all printed literature and theology) and all agree! Why? The apostle Peter answers this question for us: 'Holy men of God spoke as they were moved by the Holy Spirit' (2 Peter 1:21). Because of the Spirit's immediate divine revelation the Old Testament prophets and New Testament writers were inspired to pen the Bible's 66 books now sufficient, authoritative and complete. The Holy Scriptures are central to the Christian faith and the authentic Word of God has been preserved in God's providence whole and sufficient to make us wise unto salvation. Calvin is firm on this, and clarifies the preachers' role:

Let us remember, however, that the authority which Scripture attributes to pastors is wholly contained within the limits of the ministry of the Word, for the fact is that Christ has not given this authority to men, but to the Word of which He has made these men servants ... If they should ever turn away from that Word in order to follow the fancies and inventions of their own heads, then they are no longer to be received as pastors; they are, rather, pernicious wolves who are to be chased away! For Christ has laid down that we should not listen to anybody except those who teach us what they have taken from His Word.[82]

The New Testament authors continually refer to the Old Testament as Scripture, labelling it the oracles of God (2 Timothy 3:16; 2 Peter 1:21).

---

82 John Calvin, *Truth for all Time* (Edinburgh: The Banner of Truth Trust, 1998), pp. 123–125.

It can be seen that certain Old Testament passages and themes keep on recurring in the New Testament corpora. The writers were aware that they stood *under the authority* and testimony of Old Testament covenant documents which were sacred Scripture. The New Testament authors were men whose minds were opened by the Holy Spirit. The ancient Old Testament texts proved to the New Testament writers that Jesus of Nazareth really did fulfil prophecy, yet it was only after Pentecost the work of the Holy Spirit anointed the New Testament writers (under direct divine inspiration) to tell their contemporaries (and their successors) the story of Jesus the Messiah (John 17:5; 20:30–31). Thus the New Testament was written when by the Spirit of God the Old Testament became clear (Ephesians 3:3–6; 1:9–12). This leads us to the positive conclusion that the whole Bible is timeless, trustworthy, and will have a transforming consequence on all who read and believe. When we grasp that God is the Potentate of history, and history is the working out of His decrees, we will interpret the acts of God with understanding and speak 'thus says the Lord' faithfully as ambassadors and heralds.

Unconditional election

This is a topic shared in both Testaments and is made clearer in the New Testament. Did Jesus speak of it? Three clear examples stand out: Matthew (22:14): 'For many are called, but few are chosen'; John (15:16): 'You did not choose Me, but I chose you and appointed you that you should go and bear fruit'; and John (17:2): 'As many as you have given Him'. This latter phase is repeated almost identically another five times in His John 17 prayer (vv. 6, 9, 11, 12, 24) and it points to the doctrine of election. There are other various texts and portions of Scripture which speak of the doctrine.

Paul makes it clear in Ephesians 1:4–5: 'He chose us in Him before the foundation of the world … having predestined us to adoption as sons … according to the good pleasure of His will,' while in verse 9 we read of

'His good pleasure which He purposed in Himself ... being predestined'. This makes the doctrine clear and shows us that:

- The sovereignty of God is spoken in the words *'He chose us'*.

- The election of God is revealed here, *'having predestined us'*.

- The *'good pleasure'* of God is preached here. God looks into Himself and chooses a holy seed (v. 9).

- The gift of God is salvation, 'and that not of yourselves; it is the gift of God' (Ephesians 2:8).

The best way to see this truth is through the eyes of Romans chapters 8 and 9. There Paul places the doctrine of election and its corollary predestination in a pastoral setting. He calls the saved 'God's elect' (8:33). How are the elect saved? He lists the process in (8:28–30). We call it the 'Chain of Salvation':

For whom He foreknew, He also predestined to be conformed to the image of His Son, that He might be the firstborn among many brethren. Moreover whom He predestined, these He also called; whom He called, these He also justified; and whom He justified, these He also glorified.

Election is the decree of God which determines our destiny. He has chosen some from all the fallen of mankind to be the undeserving objects of His love. Predestination (Greek *pro-oridzō*) is the means by which that destiny is realised with God bringing to pass all necessary events and measures. 'Whom He did foreknow' (Greek *proginoskō*, lit. 'to know before') hints at something personal. The text does not say, *'what* He did foreknow' but *'whom* He did foreknow' (cf. 'I have loved you with an everlasting love; therefore with lovingkindness I have drawn you' (Jeremiah 31:3). Pastors are to reject hyper-Calvinism and are to explain the difference between the two.[83] Our Protestant Confession and Catechisms are more than helpful for understanding this mystery; '(All) those whom God has predestined unto life (and those only), He is pleased in His appointed and accepted time, effectually to call, by His Word and Spirit out of a state of sin and death.'[84] The Westminster Confession, *Shorter Catechism* Q. 20, asks and answers: 'Did God leave all mankind to perish in the estate of sin and misery?' Answer: 'God having out of His mere good pleasure, from all eternity, elected some to everlasting life ... to bring them into a state of salvation by a Redeemer.'

The necessity of saving faith

It is clear in both Testaments that righteousness by faith brings salvation was in the promise of mercy for Israel (Genesis 4:4; Psalm 103:17; Romans 4:3; Hebrews 11:4–5). The phrase 'the just shall live by faith' (Habakkuk 2:4) is repeated twice in the New Testament as clear evidence of the necessity of saving faith in the Old and New dispensations and that it is God's way of salvation in both (Romans 1:17; Hebrews 10:37–39). The book of Hebrews tells us that the faith seen in the Israelites was a present and a saving grace, and the true seed and the true Israel are those who believe the gospel and abide in the Vine (Hebrews 11:3,17–22; John 15:1–10; Romans 4:9–18; 9:6f; Galatians 3:14f, 29; 6:16; Ephesians 2:11ff, 3:6–8).

---

83 Hyper-Calvinism distinguishes itself from traditional Calvinism as regards the 'sufficiency and efficiency' of Christ's atonement. It denies there is a free offer, a duty of faith and duty of repentance and that there is such a thing as 'common grace'. Also that God has any sort of love for the non-elect. So a Hyper-Calvinist is one who goes beyond and over the bounds of what Calvinism teaches (and thus over the bounds of what the Bible teaches). He is excessive in his application of the doctrines. This manifests itself in an over-emphasis of one aspect of God's character at the expense of another. (Cf. https://www.challies.com/articles/hyper-calvinism-a-brief-definition/).

84 Westminster Confession, chapter 10, para. 1. Also, London Baptist Confession 1689, chapter 10, para. 1).

Without faith it is impossible to please Him, for he who comes to God must believe that He is, and that He is a rewarder of those who diligently seek Him. (Hebrews 11:6)

Calvin defines faith as a 'firm and sure knowledge of the divine favour toward us, founded on the truth of a free promise in Christ, and revealed to our minds, and sealed in our hearts, by the Holy Spirit' (*Institutes*, 3:2:7 & 9; cf. 3:2:15). Jesus Christ is the object of saving faith. It is not a commitment to certain truths about Christ but a commitment to Christ Himself. Faith brings about personal union with Christ and is the conviction that I am no longer in a state of nature but in a state of grace. Faith is not belief that we have been saved but it is given to trust in Christ *in order* to be saved. Faith proceeds from the conviction that we are lost. Faith is the direct activity of a regenerate heart with Christ as its object. Evangelicals teach that salvation is by faith *alone* in Jesus Christ. Salvation is not gained by good works or by being good or by doing penance and partaking of sacraments; rather it belongs to all who believe the gospel message from whatever background and who put their trust in Jesus Christ alone for salvation (Romans 5:1; Philippians 3:9). These convictions flow from the enlightened and regenerate mind (Romans 12:1–2) through the sovereign work of God the Spirit in the soul. Conversion is not to be compared to falling in love (and out again), or a drug-induced trip (hallucination), or a dream. Conversion is not from me or by me but from God. Nor is it because of education but the result of illumination, nor rooted in culture but in calling. Not existential but spiritual. Get it?! 'You must be born again.'

God and covenant promises

God's covenants are monergistic.[85] With Israel, God made an agreement that if they kept His laws (moral, civil and ceremonial) He would bless

---

85 Monergism: 'In Scripture God's covenants with men are always sovereign administrations of grace and of promise' (John Murray, 'Covenant', *The New Bible Dictionary* (London: IVP, 1970).

them. They, however, did not do so and were chastened and eventually scattered amongst all the nations of the earth (Nehemiah 9; cf. Acts 7). Monergistic covenants are those which God has made with Himself (Hebrews 6:17–18) and he is utterly committed to keeping the promises to all who have believed His Word in whatever economy they find themselves, whether Old or New; He cannot lie, He is always faithful to Himself:

If we deny Him, He also will deny us. If we are faithless, He remains faithful; He cannot deny Himself. (2 Timothy 2:12b–13)

The covenant of grace with mankind continues to the end of time and was made between the Father and the Son before the creation. Jesus Christ was the subject and Surety (i.e. one legally responsible for our debts) of the covenant. All God's promises were concerning Him and all the benefits were provided because of Him. As Surety, He undertook all that was required by the terms of the covenant and 'to affect it by His Spirit and grace'.[86] God made a covenant of works with Adam, 'with a prescription of duties and promise of reward'.[87] Thereafter with Noah (Genesis 6:18; 9:9–17); Abraham (Genesis 15; 17; 22:15–18); Israel via Moses (Exodus 2:24–25; 20:1–17); David (Psalm 89:3–4, 26–27; 132:11–18). The last was messianic in its ultimate reference (Acts 2:30–36; 1 Corinthians 11:25). Most Christians know nothing of this reality. However, we owe everything to the covenants of God, as Spurgeon said:

Christians love to think of God's covenant. All the power, all the grace, all the blessings, all the mercies, all the comforts, all the things we have, flow to us from the well-head, through the covenant. If there were no covenant, then we should fail indeed; for all grace proceeds from it, as light and heat from the sun. No angels

---

86 John Owen, *Works*, Vol. 18, pp. 78ff.
87 Ibid.

ascend or descend, save upon that ladder which Jacob saw, at the top of which stood a covenant God.[88]

God's promises are His responses to our needs. God's providential and spiritual care for His people flows from His promised oath (Hebrews 6:17–18). In John 17 the Saviour refers back to the promise made to Him by the Father in the covenant of grace. As the Surety of the covenant He asks for His promised reward (John 17:24). John Owen says that upon the accomplishment of Jesus' duties He made His request, and expected that the promises given to Him in the covenant should be made good and fulfilled, 'being made unto Him and being confirmed with the oath of God' (Hebrews 7:20; 12:2).[89] Here is a new covenant. This is also called *better* because it brings a better hope to believers than was given to Israel, and was secured by a *better sacrifice* (Hebrews 7:19,22,27). Two covenants: this is why the Reformers and their successors the Puritans (both English and Scottish) speak in their writings of the 'Covenant of Grace'[90] or, as the book of Hebrews calls it, 'the everlasting covenant' (Hebrews 13:20; 8:7).

Those who divide the world's history into seven dispensations appear to forget the covenants and Paul's gospel (2 Corinthians 3:6–18) which goes back to Adam and Abraham recognising that the Mosaic covenant was for Israel and is done away with as a way of salvation while the Ten Commandments remain valid as the Moral Law and as the way of holy living for all who believe (i.e. all who are justified by faith alone).

The priesthood of all believers

Old Testament worship was regulated through the functions of the Levitical priesthood. However, in the New Testament era, Jesus Christ

---

88 C. H. Spurgeon, *Morning & Evening*, February 22, 'The mighty God of Jacob', Genesis 49:24.
89 Ibid.
90 Cf. John Murray, 'Covenant', *The New Bible Dictionary* (London: IVP, 1970).

is the church's High Priest (Romans 8:34; Hebrews 8:1–6) and on the cross He offered Himself as a spotless sacrifice to God to atone for sins not His own and He is now at the right hand of God in heaven, praying for us (Ephesians 5:2; Hebrews 9:24–28). As a result, it is possible to come to God the Father only through Christ Jesus the Son, and only because of this mediation (Romans 8:34; John 14:6); there is no room for other mediators.[91] There has been a change in the priesthood since the cross (Hebrews 7:12; 8:6). New Testament Christians should regard themselves as a body of holy priests made up from all the people of God (1 Peter 2:4, 9–10). Evangelical Protestants believe that God takes the initiative in salvation because of His love for the elect. In fact, without this divine initiative in grace, all are powerless and lost. This grace we call 'special' or 'evangelical' grace, as opposed to 'common' grace which is experienced by all. It is God's grace that calls us into the priesthood of all believers. The doctrine of the priesthood of all believers is the distinctive feature of Protestantism, it being rooted in the believer's justification and adoption, and it is found throughout the Bible. In Christ we have become, through salvation, kings and priests, 'to offer up spiritual sacrifices acceptable to God through Jesus Christ' (1 Peter 2:5, 9–10; Romans 12:1; 15:15–16; Hebrews 13:15–16; Revelation 1:6). The doctrine of the priesthood of all believers says the born-again believer now has the privilege of going directly to God in prayer without earthly or other mediators. This is why the Christian's prayers have power with God. Roman Catholics deny this and thus they relegate the laity to a second-class status. Not only so, but they deny to the Christian a personal relationship with God through Jesus Christ that needs no formal or popish priesthood (1 John 1:7). The doctrine of the

---

91 The universal influence of the Roman Catholic Church and its incorrect definition of 'a saint' have pervaded humankind. Its veneration of defied human beings is idolatry. To pray to the Virgin Mary seriously ignores the mediatorial office and work of our Saviour and His continuing intercession for His Church. We are not instructed anywhere in Scripture to pray to Mary or angels. Jesus gave instruction to us to pray to the Father, 'in His name'.

priesthood of all believers encourages freedom in prayer, helped by the Holy Spirit, on the basis of the merits of Christ alone.[92]

Reformation history and doctrine

Protestant Reformation history and theology is not to be neglected. The Reformation was ignited in October 1517 when Martin Luther, a German Augustinian friar, published his Ninety-Five Theses. These were nailed to a church door in the university town of Wittenberg by Luther himself. Luther's propositions challenged the errors and practices of Roman Catholic doctrine and were mainly criticising common church practice of the day: the selling of indulgences.[93] To Luther, this was tantamount to selling salvation, something that was against biblical teaching. At the time Rome was using the sale of indulgences as a means to raise money for a massive new church project: the construction of St Peter's Basilica. This said, we need to preach and teach that it was a movement that was born via the Spirit of God in sixteenth-century Europe while remembering that the gospel was always present and preserved where the Bible was known and believed. Men like John Huss in Bohemia, John Wycliffe in England, as well as remnants of Celtic Christianity in Scotland and Ireland and separated believers in other parts of Europe were always true to the gospel message as much as they were able. Luther's Ninety-Five Theses were the challenge to the papacy and it lit a great fire which is still burning and spreading light in the entire world. The Reformation in Europe was established and the Evangelical and Reformed church sprang up. Today (Wikipedia says) over 33,000 Protestant denominations believe in the priesthood of all believers and hold the Bible as the supreme authority in matters of faith, doctrine and morals.

---

92 For a fuller treatment, see my book *Getting to Grips with Prayer: its Reality, Challenges and Potential* (Leominster: Day One, 2017), chapter 5.

93 Pope Leo X (11 December 1475 – 1 December 1521), born Giovanni di Lorenzo de' Medici, was pope from 9 March 1513 to his death.

10. What to preach (2)

'The studious, thoughtful Christian is always more unworldly and sincere than the Christian who reads but little and thinks still less.' (W. G. T. Shedd)[94]

'I cannot speak without a text.' (D. Martyn Lloyd-Jones, *Knowing the Times*, p. 198)[95]

'For I am not ashamed of the gospel of Christ, for it is the power of God to salvation for everyone who believes, for the Jew first and also for the Greek. For in it the righteousness of God is revealed from faith to faith; as it is written, "The just shall live by faith."' (Romans 1:16–17)

'Preach the word! Be ready in season and out of season. Convince, rebuke, exhort, with all longsuffering and teaching.' (2 Timothy 4:2)

The message of the gospel has come to us through Jesus Christ (Hebrews 1:1–4) and is preserved in the Bible for all humankind to read. There Jesus Christ is proclaimed as the only Mediator between God and those made in His image (Acts 4:12). Jesus exercised a preaching and teaching ministry and the church has followed in His steps. It is incumbent on all the people of God to say what He said and teach what the Bible makes clear, i.e. that Jesus Christ is the only Saviour (John 3:16–17).

---

94 W. G. T. Shedd, *Homiletics and Pastoral Theology*, pp. 284–285.
95 Sargent, *Gems from Martyn Lloyd-Jones*, p. 234.

Pastors must stay faithful to the revelation of Jesus Christ, God's Son, the Saviour in all His completeness and saving presentation. They must not remain silent even in today's pluralistic society because Christians are convinced that 'faith comes by hearing, and hearing by the Word of God' (Romans 10:17), and while believing that the Word of God is living and powerful, the redeemed pastor/preacher must continue to 'preach the word in season and out of season' being always dependent on the Holy Spirit for grace and strength and open doors. The phrase *'rightly dividing the word of truth'* has been used to circulate views of Scripture that are, in my opinion, not valid as an understanding of the whole of God's plan and dealings with the world and the redeemed church, views that do not aid the presentation of the gospel truth or intellectual thoroughness. It is therefore incumbent on those who are serious about providing, proclaiming and protecting the biblical message that they do not neglect the Reformation Confessions of Faith for sources of clear and considered theology and soteriology (these are the product of a mature Protestant theology a hundred years after the Reformation). The Reformed pastor/preacher is to hold and preach reformed theology. He must avoid Antinomianism, Arianism (including Modalism[96]), Arminianism, Dispensationalism, Hyper-Calvinism, Romanism, Unitarianism, and all that oppose salvation by free grace alone through faith alone in Jesus Christ alone.

---

96 *Modalism* teaching on the Trinity denies the permanence of the three Persons; Father, Son and Holy Spirit. It promotes a teaching that each Person is a temporary manifestation of existence and that the Son is identified with the Father and that, 'in the Godhead the only differentiation was a mere succession of modes or operations. The result of their doctrine is that the Father suffered as the Son. This is similar to the Arian view condemned at the Council of Nicaea, 325 AD. To quote Henry Bettenson, 'the Father Himself into the virgin, was Himself born of her, Himself suffered: in fact that He Himself was Jesus Christ' (*Documents of the Christian Church*, London: Oxford University Press, 1974, p. 38f). It was opposed by Tertullian (325 AD) and condemned as heresy by the Chalcedon Creed in 451 AD. It still exists today, especially in Pentecostalism (*Oneness Pentecostalism*, in 'Dictionary of Pentecostalism and Charismatic Movements', Eds. S. M. Burgess and G. B. McGee; Grand Rapids, MI, Zondervan Publishing House, 1995).

The Reformed faith

The term *Protestant* grew out of the Reformation and was first used in Germany 1539. It was synonymous with *Reformed* in Switzerland and France and used widely in the seventeenth century onwards.[97] The designation *Protestantism* is used to signify Christians who reject the Roman Catholic and Orthodox Church theology. Protestants accept only two sacraments, viz. baptism in the name of the Holy Trinity and the Lord's Supper.

We believe that the Protestant Reformation was driven forward by the Holy Spirit. This was accompanied, in God's providential timing, with the invention of the printing press (1440) and the discovery of the manuscripts of the New Testament which were republished (between 1514 and 1641) and then translated into the vernacular for the populace to read. As in the days of Ezra, when the Word of God was rediscovered, the Holy Scriptures became a mighty force for the revival of the church and the restoration of truths that had been lost or corrupted. Therefore, in sixteenth-century Europe there was light given again upon the Word of God. This revealed the gift of faith and the true knowledge of the gospel. It changed hearts and many were stirred to reform the church and proclaim the gospel of free grace for all. Martyrdom did not stop the progress of Holy Spirit empowered preaching and the necessary political reform required to bring about Reformation in the United Kingdom and in other parts of Europe.

Evangelical Protestants still believe today:

1. SOLA SCRIPTURA

This entails the conviction that God's truth is supremely revealed through His Word in both Testaments (of 66 books), and that the Bible truth must always take precedence over reason, tradition, ecclesiastical authority and individual experience. *Sola Scriptura* is foundational and so much so that even today's liberal Protestants (who do not believe in inerrancy of the

---

97 *Chambers Dictionary of Etymology*, 2008.

Scriptures) still take the Bible as the basis of their faith in spite of rejecting its infallibility. The early churches of the Reformation period believed the Bible was a source of authority higher than that of Church tradition.[98] Sadly, the Roman Church has added other spurious dogmas since the Reformation; for example, the Immaculate Conception, the Assumption of the Virgin Mary and the doctrine of Papal Infallibility are well-known.

2. SOLA GRATIA

Protestants believe that God takes the initiative in salvation because of His love for the elect. In fact, without this divine initiative in grace, all are sinners and lost. Grace flows from the mercy and pity of God Himself. This grace we call 'special or evangelical grace' as opposed to common grace experienced by all people, and thus salvation by grace alone, for 'by grace we are saved' (Ephesians 2:8–9). Protestants reject the idea that divine grace comes through the hands of a special priesthood, believing rather it to be a gift of God that bears the fruit of holy living. God's grace calls us into the universal priesthood of all believers. It implies the right and duty of Christians not only to read the Bible in the vernacular but also to take part in the government and all the public affairs of the local churches. It is opposed to the hierarchical system which puts power and authority in an exclusive priesthood ('bishops' etc.) and makes ordained priests the necessary and only mediators between God and His people. However, a universal priesthood allows for a common dignity, calling and sonship of all believers before God, who are described in the New Testament as kings and priests before God (1 Peter 2:9; Revelation 1:6; 5:10). They are able and required to offer up spiritual sacrifice to God (Hebrews 13:15–16: Romans 15:15–16). This is why the Christian's prayers have power with God.

---

98 'The first generation of Protestants regarded an appeal to the supreme authority of the Bible as both theologically correct and ecclesiastically liberating', Alister McGrath, *Christianity's Dangerous Idea* (New York: Harper One, 2007), p. 201.

3. SOLA FIDE

It is faith alone that brings us into a right standing with God when we are saved by grace through faith in Christ Jesus alone. Protestantism holds that faith justifies and declares us righteous in God's sight. Martin Luther after his conversion said: 'Justification by faith only is the faith of a standing or falling Church.' The Larger Catechism set out the doctrine in short compass:

Justification is an act of God's free grace unto sinners, in which He pardons all their sins, accepts and accounts their persons righteous in His sight; not for anything wrought in them, or done by them, but only for the perfect obedience and full satisfaction of Christ, by God imputed to them, and received by faith alone.[99]

Justification by faith alone gives us acceptance, cleansing and adoption. This is solid biblical ground and it must be preached to all nations and in all continents. A diligent reader of the Scriptures will know that *'the just shall live by his faith'* (Habakkuk 2:4c). Verse 4c is quoted three times in the New Testament. The doctrine goes well with the gospel emphases of Paul (Romans 1:17; Galatians 3:11; Hebrews 10:38) and also in Hebrews 11:6 that:

without faith it is impossible to please Him, for he who comes to God must believe that He is, and that He is a rewarder of those who diligently seek Him.

So the Spirit's witness is a divine testimony given to the soul. In these verses we find the word *marturia* several times. It gives us the English word 'martyr', i.e. 'a witness; someone who bears testimony or gives evidence' (vb. *martureo*).

By faith 'the elders obtained a *good* testimony' (Hebrews 11:2). This speaks of the inner witness of the Holy Spirit when one believes and is

---

99 Westminster Confession of Faith 'Larger Catechism' Q. 70, 'What is justification?' (c. 1647).

reckoned righteous by God (cf. Hebrews 10:15; 11:2,4,5). Those converted persons (saints) now possess a personal assurance aiding new trust and encouraging a desire for holiness. Saving faith justifies (declares us righteous) and also sanctifies (set us apart) because righteousness is both imputed and imparted at conversion, and thus the righteousness of the law is 'fulfilled in us who do not walk according to the flesh but according to the Spirit' (Romans 8:4).

4. SOLUS CHRISTUS

Jesus Christ is the Citadel of Christianity, that is, He is its heart, object, joy, peace, foundation, and eternal guarantee of full salvation. Without Him there is no redemption, no forgiveness and no acceptance with God. Christians recognise Him as the Saviour of the world and boldly declare that 'He alone became the son of Man, in order that we might become through Him sons of God.'[100] The Jesus Christ of the Gospels with its genealogies, miracles and teachings and Old Testament prophecies is the only Christ the world has. If we reject this evidence we reject God's incarnate Son and the offer of eternal life (1 John 4:1–3). We must believe in the Christ child's incarnation and receive Him as 'the way, the truth, and the life' (John 14:6). His deity, His glory, His grace, His death and resurrection and ascension into heaven are all relevant to our full salvation and the gospel defined. He alone is the Redeemer and the source of eternal salvation. The eternal Sonship of Jesus Christ as the Son of God is taught everywhere in the Bible. Not only this, but those things that establish Christ's credentials as the only begotten of the Father full of grace and truth proclaim His co-equality with the Father and the Holy Spirit in Trinitarian unity; and proclaim why Jesus *only*, for no other could have done what the Son achieved by His miraculous incarnation, atoning death and third day resurrection, ascension into heaven and His continuing high priesthood ministry:

---

100 Augustine of Hippo, *A Treatise against Two Letters of the Pelagians.*

He is also able to save to the uttermost those who come to God through Him, since He always lives to make intercession for them. (Hebrews 7:25)

5. SOLI DEO GLORIA

'Salvation is of the LORD' (Jonah 2:9) because God makes us willing in the day of His power and grace. The Holy Spirit opens hearts and gives faith to believe (Lydia and Cornelius were people of prayer but were not saved until they were *born again* (cf. Acts 16). God takes the initiative in salvation but expects a believing response to the gospel and its free offer. God does not believe for us but He commands every one everywhere to repent (Acts 17:30). He has no grandchildren. Each sinner must come in repentance and faith personally to the cross to know cleansing, justification, acceptance and covenant promise. Faith and conviction of sin follows regeneration. For the theologian Louis Berkhof, 'The Being of God does not admit any scientific definition.' That is because His essential Being is hidden from us, yet we are not ignorant of God's character for we have the Bible. The Old Testament tells us that God is the *'I AM WHO I AM'* (Exodus 3:14), thus revealing that He is self-existent, self-contained and has absolute independence, while the New Testament reveals that *'God is Spirit'* (John 4:24). The early Church Fathers, because of the transcendence of God, felt that it was impossible to gain an adequate knowledge of the divine essence. The Protestant Reformers agreed that the essence of God is incomprehensible, but they did not exclude knowledge of it. They stated the *unity, simplicity,* and *spirituality* of God. So God in His Being is incomprehensible (Job 11:7), immaterial (John 4:24) and unchangeable (Exodus 3:14–15).

Pastors should preach remembering that they are called and what is expected of them: 'Be diligent to present yourself approved to God, a worker who does not need to be ashamed, rightly dividing the word of truth' (2 Timothy 2:15). It is a pastor's responsibility to correctly handle 'the word of truth'. The composite verb 'dividing' (*orthotomeō*) indicates cutting a straight line, that is handling the Scriptures aright so the Word is understood and the story of redemption is made clear. Diligent study is necessary to meet the contemporary challenges of the day; this will be partly achieved by an initial theological training (in my opinion essential so the pastor is be able to preach the whole counsel of God). The pastor is to come to his task as a Bible student and also a student of history. Church History and the Doctrine of Providence are also helpful subjects and a grasp of them will aid and clarify sermon content when required.

Preachers as preachers must emphasise:

1. THE BIBLE IS GOD-GIVEN

The Bible is under attack; but what is new? There have always been doubters and unbelievers, some of whom are determined to do what they can to devalue or destroy the Bible and the truth it proclaims, the truth about 'one God and one Mediator between God and men, the Man Christ Jesus'. They will not succeed. The eternal truth is not for sale. Nor are the 66 Books changeable or irrelevant but rather are needed and dependable, and so it is essential that we put our faith in the message of the Bible, which is that God is love and Jesus Christ is the only Saviour (1 John 5:9–12). There is no Jesus other than the Jesus of the Scriptures. If we reject Him we cannot be saved from sin and the fires of hell. It is good to declare that there are more existing manuscripts upholding the Bible's content and accuracy than for any other ancient writings.[101] We believe therefore, 'God has revealed Himself in the Bible, which consists of the Old and New Testaments alone. Every word was inspired by God through human authors, so that the Bible as originally given is in its entirety the Word of God, without error and fully reliable in fact and doctrine.'[102]

---

101 See my book, *Engaging with Islam: An Evangelical Doctrinal Perspective*, Appendix 5, 'Manuscript evidence for superior New Testament reliability (Leominster: Day One, 2019), pp. 199ff.

102 The FIEC Statement of Faith: point 1.

The Bible is one holy Book, comprising 66 books written over 1,600 years by about 40 authors, containing one message about God, Jesus Christ and the church. In the last 250 years there have been humanists, rationalists, and evolutionists, to name but a few, who are intent on challenging the authority and authenticity of the Scriptures. The philosophers David Hume (1711–1776) and Voltaire (Francois-Marie Arouet, 1694–1778) both criticised organised religion and its appeal to the supernatural. Others have done the same. Charles Darwin (1809–1882) and his theory of evolution have done so much damage to the nation's faith in God and the Bible's reputation. Jacques Derrida (1930–2004), the French philosopher, with his post-modern philosophy, which denies objective truth, has confused thousands of university students. Richard Dawkins and his book *The God Delusion* is full of invective toward God, Christ and the Bible in a vain attempt to kill off true religion. These men are today's heroes, but they will soon be tomorrow's memories when their work and ideas are seen to be unrealistic and unhelpful. In the Gospel of John, chapter 17:14, Christ says that He has given the disciples the Father's Word. He returns to that thought in verse 17 and then makes a memorable statement about the Bible, saying '*Your word is truth.*' Some look for truth through the autonomy of human reason (Benedictus de Spinoza) or human experience (Frederick Schleiermacher) and some consider that 'objective true knowledge is impossible'; Emmanuel Kant said: 'No one has the truth, but we all have an opinion.' Such an attitude and belief is contrary to the teaching of the Bible and the Reformed Confessions. Gospel truth is not found in human reason or experience but in divine wisdom. Jesus clears up any misunderstanding as to what *truth* really is. He says it is God's Word (John 17:17).

2. JESUS CHRIST'S ATONING DEATH AND BODILY RESURRECTION *ARE* THE GOSPEL

These are not 'take it or leave it' doctrines! The worship of God goes right back to Genesis and to Adam who met with God in the garden in the cool of the day. After the Fall this changed and men required an atoning sacrifice and an imputed righteousness before communion with God was possible. This was illustrated by the tunics made from the skins of animals, which God provided for Adam and Eve (Genesis 3:21). Following this, Abel offered a righteous sacrifice while Cain's attempt was refused by God (Genesis 4:1–5; Hebrews 11:4). This reinforces the need to approach God through atoning blood of Jesus Christ. Those who see Genesis 1–11 as myth (and sadly there are many in the churches who think this way) oppose the Bible's message of substitutionary atonement and the vicarious work of Jesus Christ on the cross, for Christ Jesus is 'the Mediator of the new covenant, and to the blood of sprinkling that speaks better things than that of Abel' (Hebrews 12:24). The Bible's gospel glorifies God the Father, through the Son Jesus Christ and reveals God's love and mercy to a fallen world. Christ Jesus rose from the dead on the third day to declare that He is the Son of God and the Saviour of the world (John 14:6; Acts 4:12; Hebrews 1:2). To the Greeks and the early Gnostics the idea of bodily resurrection was outlandish and incompatible with their own philosophical ideas (Acts 17:32). To them a man's body was only an evil (*kakov*) or a fetter (*desmos*) or a dungeon or grave (*swma-sema*; 'body tomb') from which death frees the soul.[103] Paul rejected these ideas and argues for Christian hope. The implication of rejecting the resurrection of Jesus on the third day is gargantuan. To deny its reality is gospel-denying and faith-destroying, cf. 1 Corinthians 15: 'If there is no resurrection of the dead, then Christ is not risen' (v. 13) 'And if Christ is not risen, then our preaching is empty and your faith is also empty' (v. 14).

Resurrection is the triumph of Jesus Christ over 'the last enemy' death (1 Corinthians 15:26). Because of this, believers can be confident that they will rise as He did on the last day. Christ has defeated Satan, who had the power of death. This power was taken from Satan at the cross (Colossians 2:14; Hebrews 2:14–15). When the resurrection day arrives,

---

103 R. C. H. Lenski, *1 & 2 Corinthians* (Minneapolis, Mi: Augsburg Publishing House, 1963), p. 624.

believers will be given bodies like that of the risen Saviour; these new bodies will be perfect, fitted for a spiritual existence and with the power of an endless life (1 Corinthians 15:50–55). Here is the solution to death and its humiliation. Those who believe the words, 'I am the resurrection and the life' (John 11:25) will share in Christ's everlasting victory. Pastors must oppose all attempts to deny, invalidate or rewrite the resurrection accounts as found in the four Gospels. Such attempts are common today, with, for example, increasing amounts of literature being produced by Islamic sources to discredit the four historical accounts in the Gospels. One such effort is centred on the New Testament phrase 'the sign of the prophet Jonah' (this saying is exploited by Muslims to deny the resurrection of our Saviour on the third day).[104]

3. JESUS CHRIST IS THE ONLY HEAD OF THE CHURCH

The Gospel of Matthew presents the historical Jesus' credentials as the Jewish Old Testament Messiah, 'the son of David, the son of Abraham' and the Saviour of the world (1:1; 28:19–20) and presents a valid Christology to those who anticipated the Old Testament Messiah as an earthy liberator from oppression. The revelation of Jesus of Nazareth as Immanuel, that is, 'God with us', is made clear as the gospel. Matthew wrote before the destruction of Jerusalem in AD 70 and he speaks of the customs of the Jews as continuing until 'this day' (27:8; 28:15). This Jesus presented is also as the apostle John the evangelist made clear:

Jesus said to him, 'I am the way, the truth, and the life. No one comes to the Father except through Me.' (John 14:6)

Who is a liar but he who denies that Jesus is the Christ? He is antichrist who denies the Father and the Son. (1 John 2:22)

---

104 See my books, *The Real Lord's Prayer* and *Engaging with Islam*, Day One Publications.

There is no priest or prophet greater than Jesus Christ. He died on the cross to save us from our sins, opening the gate to eternal life which is freely offered in the gospel. He spoke the words of God His Father which regulates the church's faith and practice. The four Gospels and the New Testament epistles declare He is the historic Jesus of Nazareth who by His incarnation is Immanuel—'God with us'—and our Prophet, Priest and King (Hebrews 1). Islam's rejection of Christ Jesus' death and third-day resurrection attacks the heart of the gospel and challenges all gospel preachers and teachers to make the claims of the historic Jesus clear and irrefutable. Salvation is not gained by good works or by doing penance and partaking of sacraments; rather it belongs to all, from whatever background, who believe the gospel message and put their trust in Jesus Christ alone for salvation in fear and with faith (Romans 5:1; Philippians 3:9). This is in sharp contrast to Roman Catholic dogma which calls on its members to trust and hope in the Church's sacrament to save their souls.

4. THE NECESSITY OF EXPERIMENTAL RELIGION IN THE SOUL

Evangelicals speak openly about the *new birth*, claiming to be *born again*. It comes from the Gospel of John chapter 3. Jesus said to the scholar Nicodemus, 'You must be born again,' and so we believe in its necessity. This is a subjective work of the Holy Spirit so overpowering and life-changing that evangelicals in all denominations lay claim to the experience—it is a shared mantra. It is not an optional extra but the beginning of all saving work in the soul. Protestant evangelicals believe in the necessity of the new birth and its fruits of repentance and faith for salvation.

I say to you, unless one is born again, he cannot see the kingdom of God … That which is born of the flesh is flesh, and that which is born of the Spirit is spirit. Do not marvel that I said to you, 'You must be born again.' (John 3:3,6–7)

Chapter 10

Much error is extant about the nature and necessity of regeneration leading to conversion of the soul unto life eternal and its preceding enlightenment and peace with God which lets the light of the gospel be witnessed among one's contemporaries:

You are the light of the world. A city that is set on a hill cannot be hidden. Nor do they light a lamp and put it under a basket, but on a lampstand, and it gives light to all who are in the house. Let your light so shine before men, that they may see your good works and glorify your Father in heaven. (Matthew 5:14–16)

11. Public worship

> 'The acceptable way of worshipping the true God is instituted
> by Himself and so limited by His own revealed will, that He
> may not be worshipped according to the imagination and
> devices of men, nor the suggestions of Satan, under any visible
> representations, or any other way not prescribed in the Holy
> Scriptures.' (Westminster Confession of Faith, chapter 21:1)

'You shall worship the Lord your God and Him only shall you serve.'
(Matthew 4:10)

'A son honours his father, and a servant his master. If then I am the Father,
where is My honour? And if I am a Master, where is My reverence? Says
the Lord of hosts.' (Malachi 1:6)

It is important to distinguish between public worship, personal, private and family worship. Public worship is when the gathered church is assembled to pray. We owe to God devotion and obedience in every area of our life (1 Corinthians 10:31) and we must do everything as unto Him and walk in the Spirit daily (Ephesians 5). However, the exercise of collective public worship, viz. prayer, reading the Word, preaching (from the Word), singing God's praise, the ordinances of baptism and the Lord's Supper, are all elements which distinguish between gathered church worship and what is sometime called 'fellowship hours'. The idea of duty (worship) is not popular today. So the Bible's teaching on worship appears too rigid to many contemporaries. Why should men ask God for His ideas for worship and search for His rules if that would take the fun out of the worship service when they are not happy with the way things are commanded?

The worship of God goes back to Genesis and to Adam who met God in the Garden of Eden in the cool of the day. After the Fall and the removal from paradise Abel offered righteous sacrifices while Cain's attempts were refused by God (Genesis 4:1–5; Hebrews 11:4). This reinforces the need to approach God through atoning blood. Contemporary [young] populations are demanding styles of worship unknown to our Protestant forebears and will vote with their feet, deserting the more traditional churches if unhappy: the draw and influence of modernity is powerful and few can resist it. Other factors are Bible ignorance and the hubris of youth. There is need for clear Bible knowledge on this issue. So much of what passes as contemporary worship is ruled by taste, influenced by modernity, or accepted as OK because of the appalling lack of knowledge on what the Bible instructs on the matter. Not all the churches have succumbed to the power of modernity but it would be true to say that in most instances those congregations that have not, are smaller on average than the rest. Sadly, it is the desire to be larger along with the aim of wanting to be more effective in outreach, which drives churches to move from the well-trodden precepts and practices of the Scriptures. This reflects the lack of respect for the teaching of the Word, causing a diminished role for preaching even in nonconformist churches, so much so that they are in danger of losing the voice of God to this new generation.

The object of worship is God

The first obligation for all humans is to worship and love God (Romans 1:18–25; Mark 12:30). That is the main reason for gathered worship one day in seven and following the resurrection of Jesus Christ (Revelation 1:10). Other reasons are secondary. Why do we evangelise? So that true worship among the nations is established, of course! It follows that the object of worship is God. He alone is to be worshipped: 'You shall worship the LORD your

God, and Him only you shall serve' (Matthew 4:10; cf. Revelation 11:16). But who or what is God? If I am to worship God I need to know 'what' He is. That is less known now in the UK and Europe than any time since the Reformation, since the tradition of catechising our children has fallen out of favour with the majority of Christian parents who, having succumbed to rationalist propaganda, do not catechise their offspring. The answer to the children's catechism question, 'What is God?' is unknown.[105] The Bible reveals to us the nature and essence of God Almighty. He made Himself known to Abraham and also to (the children of) Israel over thousands of years through the inspired prophets and now to the world through Jesus Christ the living Word who has declared Him (John 1:18). The Bible being the self-revelation of God, it conveys specific and wonderful information about God's Being and essence and what He requires of His people. Worship is to be regulated according to His Word. Public worship can be defined as 'the gathered church approaching God through Jesus Christ as command and directed by the Scriptures, with sincere and humble hearts lifted in praise to hear His Word in order that they may believe and obey His will'. God has disclosed Himself in creation and providence (Psalm 19; Romans 1:18–20). We learn from general revelation that God is all powerful, intelligent, wise, good and patient, and we learn from the Scriptures of the Old and New Testament 'what' and 'who' He is and what He says and requires from His redeemed people.

The theory of worship

The doctrine of worship is the application of the Reformed principle of *Sola Scriptura*. True worship may include only those matters which God has expressly commanded in Scripture or may 'be deduced by good and necessary consequence' (cf. Matthew 28:20). The Reformation was a reaction to the errors and excesses of the Roman Catholic Church that

---

105 God is a Spirit, infinite, eternal, and unchangeable, in His being, wisdom, power, holiness, justice, goodness, and truth' (Shorter Catechism, No. 4).

had over a thousand years added so much to its liturgy and practice that it had become formal and totally dependent on a priesthood which also encouraged the idolatrous adoration of its saints, contrary to Scripture. The Reformation principle is that God has revealed and prescribed what is acceptable so that the imaginations of men or the suggestions of Satan are rejected. The Baptist Confession of Faith, 1689 (chapter 22:1), 'Of Religious Worship', states:

The acceptable way of worshipping the true God is instituted by Himself and so limited by His own revealed will, that He may not be worshipped according to the imagination and devices of men, nor the suggestions of Satan, under any visible representations, or any other way not prescribed in the Holy Scriptures.

The Protestant Reformer John Calvin taught that whatever is and set forth is foundational in Reformed thinking. John Hooper's dictum, 'Anything not required by Scripture may not be required by the Church',[106] was the regulating principle that eventually held great sway among the Puritan corpus. God is pleased when the gathered church comes together to worship through Jesus Christ our High Priest who is a priest 'for ever after the order of Melchizedek' (Hebrews 5:6).

What is the best way to worship God? The New Testament makes it clear that He expects His people 'to offer up spiritual sacrifices acceptable to Him through Jesus Christ' (1 Peter 2:5). Spiritual worship is what is authorised, controlled by the Spirit and offered in faith. In the New Testament, worship in homes is acceptable (Colossians 4:15); then worship was simple and full of promise (John 9:31); love and devotion to Christ was the key. The call to assemble is seen in Hebrews (10:24–25; cf. 1 Corinthians 11:17–18; 14:26; James 2:2). The word used for church (*ecclesia*) is a gathered assembly. The prescribed day of worship *par*

---

106 James T. Dennison, *The Market Day of the Soul* (Morgan, PA: Sol Deo Gloria Publications, 2001), p. ix.

excellence was the Lord's Day (Acts 20:7; 1 Corinthians 16:1–2). The church, because of grace and truth, must worship God alone (John 4:20–24; Romans 15:5–6; 1 Peter 2:5). The people of God are known in the New Testament as 'a holy priesthood':

Chosen by God and precious, you also, as living stones, are being built up a spiritual house, a holy priesthood, to offer up spiritual sacrifices acceptable to God through Jesus Christ. (1 Peter 2:4a–5)

Worship, including prayer, praise (singing psalms, hymns and spiritual songs) and preaching are acceptable when in fellowship with God the Spirit. They are offered as holy sacrifices through His Son Jesus Christ. New Testament worship was characterised by joy and thanksgiving because of God's gracious redemption in Christ. This early Christian worship focused on God's saving work in Jesus Christ. True worship was that which occurred under the inspiration of God's Spirit (John 4:23–24; Philippians 3:3). The Jewish Sabbath was, with dominical and apostolic authority, quickly replaced by the first day Sabbath as the appointed time for weekly public worship (John 20:26; Acts 2:1; 20:7; 1 Corinthians 16:2). This was called the Lord's Day (Revelation 1:10). This was the occasion of celebration for the resurrection of Jesus, since He arose on the first day of the week (Mark 16:2).[107]

Church worship music

This can be contentious! A pastor must work with the musicians/presenters (if present) in his congregation to aid worship and lift the

---

107 Jesus called His coming resurrection the *sign of Jonah* (Matthew 12:39; 16:4; cf Luke 11:29). The *sign of Jonah* was the sign of Christ's resurrection on the third day. Thus those who keep the Lord's Day-Sabbath holy in this dispensation proclaim it as a *sign* to their own generation and the world that Christ has risen from the dead. Those who respect the Lord's Day-Sabbath testify to the world that Sunday is the special day on which the people of God are called to gather together to worship: 'If it were not for the Sabbath there would be little public and visible appearance of serving, worshipping and reverencing the supreme and invisible being.'

souls of the people to heaven in weekly praise and thanksgiving with joy. He must work with his organist/pianist with respect and patience as these matters are famous for being delicate. I have known of pastors who had to leave their churches because of conflict over the issue of new hymns, and organists over the unkindness of church leaders. It should not be presumed that musicians will take kindly to overbearing leadership. I have observed that church gifted musicians are often taken for granted and are little appreciated until they are not around! My advice is to treat them well and show them personal appreciation and church thanks. This required gratitude needs to be clearly explained to younger clergy. It is best to be 'wise as serpents and harmless as doves' (Matthew 10:16).

The blessings of public worship

Going to church on Sunday is all part of the Christian lifestyle and culture, but for some of us it is unfortunately no more than routine and for others just a necessary duty. I once spoke to a woman who wanted to come to church whenever she felt like it, but not too regularly please! But this is not the Bible's view of things. It speaks of 'not forsaking the assembling of ourselves together' (Hebrews 10:25). Clearly, the Bible expects Christians to meet together weekly. However, even in apostolic times some people obviously neglected this important weekly event!

The local church, in the New Testament, is neither a building nor a denomination but is an assembly/congregation of people gathered for a purpose—but what is that purpose? Why *do* Christians gather Sunday by Sunday? What reasons draw them together? In the book of Revelation we read of John that he was 'in the Spirit on the Lord's Day' (1:10). This day is so called because it is a special day that belongs to Christ Jesus—it bears this uniquely distinctive form of designation with 'the Lord's Supper' (1 Corinthians 11:20). So why this unusual significance, and where does it come from? The day must be so called because it follows the established designation at that time current in c.AD 98 when the book of Revelation was written. The apostle John's words in Revelation 1:10 are to be clearly understood as referring, as Hoeksema says, 'to the day of the Lord's resurrection, the first day of the week, set aside by the apostles under the direction of the Holy Spirit as a day of special worship and consecration to take the place of the seventh day sabbath of the old dispensation'.[108]

Revelation 1:10

There are four blessings of 'day one' worship signalled in Revelation 1:10:

1. HEARING THE VOICE OF CHRIST

Because John was open to the Holy Spirit he heard the voice of the risen Christ saying, 'I am the Alpha and the Omega' (vv. 10,11). The Word of God is meant to be heard in the gathered congregation. This is *the* vital element of true worship as there is a close connection between the Spirit, worship on the Lord's Day, and the Word of God.

2. UNDERSTANDING THE WORD OF GOD

Because John was 'in the Spirit', Christ speaks to him through a twofold vision. John turned to see the voice but saw the seven golden lampstands (v. 12) which in turn brought understanding of the 'One like the Son of man' (v. 13). The object that was presented to John's view needed interpretation, therefore a 'translation in the Spirit was necessary to prepare John to receive the visions'.[109] When gathered on the Lord's Day the churches are promised the Holy Spirit in support of worship (Ephesians 5:18–19). It is in the Word that we find the historic Jesus revealed and explained. It is on the Lord's Day that God promises His special presence and blessing. It was

---

108 Hoeksema, *Behold He Cometh* (Grand Rapids, MI: Reformed Free Publishing Association, 1974), p. 34
109 Ibid.

so in the old dispensation and it is still true in the New. It is by the Holy Spirit that the blessing is mediated and believers are enabled to respond to the voice of the Word.

3. RECEIVING HOPE FROM THE SCRIPTURES

When John saw the glory of the risen Christ it was all too much for him, and he 'fell at His feet as dead' (v. 17). The Lord's presence overwhelmed him and he felt humbled before the risen Christ. But the real purpose of the vision was not to terrify but to comfort. In the vision John saw the exalted Christ in relation to His church, which in the book of Revelation is presented as in a state of tribulation. John saw the things that are yet to come which pointed to the Lamb's victory and the new heavens and the new earth (v. 19).

4. RECEIVING THE SPIRIT'S HELP TO DO GOD'S WORK

Christ's voice instructs John. He asks him to write the things that he saw (v. 19). Here is the doctrine of Bible inerrancy illustrated for us. The Bible was written by 'holy men ... as they were moved by the Holy Spirit' (2 Peter 1:21). John was experiencing immediate inspiration of the Spirit. This is what renders the Bible inspired and utterly trustworthy. We learn from here also that today's saints need the Spirit's grace to equip and empower them for holy service. With that operative in their hearts God's people can obey the Word of Christ just as John did so long ago.

The mode of worship

It is worth noting what the phrase 'in the Spirit on the Lord's day' does not mean. It does not mean that John was transported to the day of Christ's Second Coming. The Greek (*te kuriake hemera*) does not support this (cf. the construction of 1 Corinthians 11:20), so the best translation is 'the Lord's Day'. It therefore does not mean 'the day of the Lord' which, in the Old Testament Greek translation of the Bible is rendered *hemera kuriou* (LXX).[110] Nor does the context support the latter idea.[111] This phrase *in the Spirit* is not an uncommon expression in Revelation (cf. 4:2; 17:3 and 21:10), but to what do these allude? Was this a 'prophetic trance' as J. R. Michaels says,[112] or was John 'in direct spiritual contact with his Saviour ... wide awake and every avenue of his soul wide open to the direct communication coming from God'?[113] The latter is the preferred option. He is awake and he is responsive to the voice of the risen Christ. It is a state in which 'the seer is especially open to the Holy Spirit'.[114] Although there is no indication that John was with a company of worshippers on the island of Patmos, we can regard him as in the attitude and spirit of worship because the Spirit governed his response to what he experiences. Are we concerned about our attitudes and spiritual health as we come to the house of God each week? We should be. These verses say to us: 'Be prepared in heart when you come to worship, and bring the Holy Spirit with you.' However, if we remain unsaved we need to go to church seeking the grace of God in the gospel for free grace salvation (Matthew 6:33; 7:7–8).

The Spirit and the Word

How does God speak to us today? Not by immediate inspiration as with the Apostle John, but with full confidence in the inerrant Scriptures through the inward witness of the Spirit. John Owen believed that the person who 'would utterly separate the Spirit from the Word had as good burn his Bible'.[115] Richard Baxter speaks of the 'concurrence' of the Spirit and the Word; it is like the male and the female; both are required together for new life. When the Spirit is involved He awakens,

---

110 The Septuagint version.
111 John Owen, says 'Nowhere; *hemera kuriake* signifies some illustrious appearance of God, in a way of judgement or mercy', *Works*, Vol. 18, p. 424.
112 J. R. Michaels, *Revelation* (Leicester: IVP, 1997), p. 59.
113 W. Hendriksen, *More than Conquerors* (London: Tyndale Press, 1973), p. 55.
114 Leon Morris, *Revelation* (Leicester: IVP, 1996), p. 52.
115 J. Owen, quoted in G. F. Nuttall, *The Holy Spirit in Puritan Faith and Experience* (Chicago: University of Chicago, 1992), p. 31.

illumines and seals the believer at conversion.[116] Calvin concurs, saying 'that the testimony of the Spirit is superior to reason. For God alone can properly bear witness to His own words, so these words will not obtain full credit in the hearts of men, until they are sealed by the inward testimony of the Spirit'.[117] The Spirit's witness is both intellectual and practical. Baxter and Owen rejected extreme ideas such as the possibility of infallible revelations. For Owen the leading of the Spirit is 'according to the *regulum*: 'the rule' (of Scripture)'. The Holy Spirit works in us 'to bring us light on the rule contained in Scripture and new power to obey its injunctions'.[118] Without the presence of the Holy Spirit there would have been no sanctified response by John to the visions he received because worship not only requires revelation but a believing response to what is heard. As believers co-operate with the Holy Spirit within them, they are sanctified through the truth (John 17:17). Thus we conclude that the Scriptures and the Spirit together are our instructors: 'God is His own interpreter and He will make it plain.' We need both the Bible and the Spirit when at worship, for we must worship God 'in spirit and in truth' (John 4:24; 17:20).

Conclusion

The spiritually blind deny God's self-disclosure and worship Him in strange ways with *strange fire*. God has given the Bible in order that we can learn what He is and what He commands. Spiritual worship also requires that we follow God's instructions. This has always been so. Worship not only requires obedience to God's will as revealed in the Scriptures, but imputed 'righteousness' because our own personal relationship must be 'right with God' (Romans 5:1). The apostle John speaks of personal and

---

116 S. Ferguson, 'John Owen and the Doctrine of the Holy Spirit', in Robert Oliver, ed. *John Owen: The Man and His Theology* (Darlington: Evangelical Press, 2002), p. 120.

117 J. Calvin, *Institutes*, 1:7:4.

118 S. Ferguson, 'John Owen and the Doctrine of the Holy Spirit', in Robert Oliver, ed. *John Owen, The Man and His Theology,* p. 120.

assured fellowship with the Father and the Son (1 John 1:3). Certainly there must be a response to the hearing of the Word of God whether read or preached. Worshippers cannot be passive or negative when it comes to honouring God. When Christians gather on the Lord's Day-Sabbath it is to worship God 'in Spirit and in truth' (John 4:24); it is wrong to try to please God in ways that are not acceptable to rule of Scripture. This rule is often called the 'Regulative Principle' and is variously interpreted in different Protestant traditions. What is sure is that the Old and New Testaments both call for obedience here as in all other things. Stephen Charnock asks, 'Could the Israelites [have] been called worshippers of God according to His order, if they had brought Him a thousand lambs that had died in a ditch or been killed at home? No. These sacrifices were to be brought to the altar alive, and their blood shed at the foot of it. A thousand sacrifices killed without had not been so valuable as one brought alive to the place of offering.'[119]

Let us ask ourselves: does our worship pass the Bible test? Is it according to the Word? Is it kept simple, spiritual, serious and scriptural? Does it engage the mind as well as the heart and emotions? Worship requires biblical warrant. Worship is a dynamic activity, but to watch some people in church you would not think that it was so! Perhaps their thoughts and affections are somewhere else? In the days of PowerPoint and online Zoom services the hymn book is not as important as it used to be, so care must be taken to sing clear and sound theology. This will preserve biblical orthodoxy. To promote unscriptural hymns and songs can imprint in the minds and hearts of the worshippers a non-biblical theology that will tend to encourage unbelief and a sentimental religiosity. It was the use of Isaac Watts' hymns in the eighteenth century that kept the Congregationalists free of the Unitarianism that invaded and ruined English Presbyterianism.

---

119 Stephen Charnock, *The Attributes of God*, Vol. 2 (London: Parsons Edition, 1815), p. 74 http://www.reformation-today.org/articles/187Psalm_139_and_the_Omniscience_of_God.pdf

Two other blessings are to be received when worshipping:

(i) Wisdom: church history tells us when God's people gathered together, they came to hear the Word of God preached. The Bible is God's divine wisdom, so worship without any reference to it is like having bread without wheat or song without words. The Bible contains the whole counsel of God and is life to the soul (Psalm 119:50). It will keep us from sin and give us an understanding of the issues of life and eternity (Proverbs 3:13). We all need to hear and receive divine wisdom and it ought to be prominent when the church gathers for worship. Jesus said: 'The words that I speak to you are spirit, and they are life' (John 6:63). Christians gather then, Sunday by Sunday, not only to sing and pray but to listen and learn also. Gathering together before a holy God, Christians yield themselves to His commands and grow in grace in the knowledge of Him: 'As newborn babes, desire the pure milk of the Word, that you may grow thereby' (1 Peter 2:2).

(ii) A welcome: feeling at home in a local church is very important to each one of us. So finding friendship, sympathy and brotherly love are vital factors in attracting us to a local place of worship. Fellowship is a very important aspect of Christian social contact, for only among God's redeemed people can believers truly feel at home. Perhaps this is why the church is called a 'spiritual house' (1 Peter 2:5). The binding command to 'love one another' (John 13:34–35) is never more appropriate than among the people of God.

12. Prayer and the local church

'Pray for what we want, and giving thanks for what we have.'
(Thomas Manton, 20 August) [120]

'When we have done with preaching, we shall not, if we are
true ministers of God, have done with praying.' (Spurgeon) [121]

'Elijah's importunate, fiery praying and God's promise brought
the rain. Prayer carried the promise to its gracious fulfilment. It
takes persistent and persevering prayer to give to the promise
its largest and most gracious results. His praying brought things
to pass. It vindicated the existence and being of God, brought
conviction to dull sluggish consciences, and proved that God
was still God in the nation.' (E. M. Bounds) [122]

It can be ascertained from the New Testament that local churches
are meant to have regular times of corporate prayer and believers
are meant to pray one with another. To neglect this fact is to miss
the blessing. Public and community times of prayer speak of life and
maturity in a local church. We remember that the incense from the
priests censer in the tabernacle consisted of various spices blended
together (Exodus 30:34–35) and it was the proper blending of one with
another that made the perfume so fragrant and refreshing. So it is that
the prayers of Paul recorded in the New Testament were full of the

---

120 Thomas Manton, from *The Puritans: Daily Readings* (Fearn: Christian Heritage, 2012), 3–6
August ff.
121 C. H. Spurgeon, *Lectures To My Students*, p. 47.
122 E. M. Bounds, *Praying and Praying Men* (Chicago: Moody Press, 1980), pp. 50–51.

ingredients necessary for holy incense, sweet and fragrant to our Father in heaven.

What should we pray? The answer is found when we examine the prayer Jesus taught, the confidence that Apostle John spoke about and Paul's intercessions for the local churches, as well as the answered prayers of the Old Testament saints (cf. Moses, Hannah, Jabez, etc.).[123]

Jesus teaches us to pray with sincere honesty

In Matthew 6 the Saviour's Lord's Prayer is a model prayer to be used both in private and public for growth of the kingdom of God on earth and for personal sanctification and perseverance. The prayer is composed of six requests: the first three ask for the kingdom to come: 'In this manner, therefore, pray: Our Father in heaven, hallowed be Your name. Your kingdom come. Your will be done on earth as it is in heaven' (vv. 9–10); and the last three are for God to meet the needs of His people until the kingdom arrives (vv. 11–13f).[124]

In this manner (v. 9) does not mean to pray using only these words, but to pray along these lines. To reduce this prayer to empty recitation is what the Lord said *not* to do (v. 7). In verse 7 the Greek pronoun translated *you* is plural. But in verse 6 it emphasises private communion with God where *you* is singular. The key to answered private prayer is to do it in secret (i.e. 'go into your room … shut your door'). 'Hallowed be Your name' (v. 9)—the verb is an imperative and means, 'May Your name be hallowed' (i.e. from the word *holy*). The hallowing of the Father's name means the realisation of His eternal existence, holiness, love, goodness, mercy and grace toward us. '*Your kingdom come*' (v. 10), is a request for blessings and salvation when the *kingdom is come* among us in saving grace and power, enabling: '*Your will be done.*' Thus we acknowledge with honest and open hearts our need of saving and persevering grace.

---

123 For Jabez see my book *Getting to grips with prayer* (Day One, 2017).
124 For Jesus' prayer in John 17, see my book *The* Real *Lord's Prayer* (Day One, 2012).

God does things in answer to prayer that He would not have done otherwise (cf. James 4:2).[125]

John encourages us to pray with confidence

The people of God who are serious about prayer wish to pray in such a way that brings assurance to the soul and receives answers.

Now this is the confidence that we have in Him, that if we ask anything according to His will, He hears us. And if we know that He hears us, whatever we ask, we know that we have the petitions that we have asked of Him. (1 John 5:14–15)[126]

John speaks here about the type of praying that God hears and answers (vv. 14–15) which the apostle James calls 'effectual prayer' (James 5:16b). However verses 16 and 17 speak of prayer which will *not* be answered because of what John calls the 'sin leading to death'. Believing prayer is very important to the life of the Christian. It remains true that believing prayer is the hand that touches Heaven's heart. However, it remains for many a paradox; yet prayer is God's idea and the 'effectual prayer' of those born of God is accepted when it flows from confidence with bold supplication. This thought is summed up in the hymn by William Cowper, 'Satan trembles when he sees the weakest saint upon his knees.'[127] These verses are about prayer that is heard by God and by implication will be answered by Him. This brings hope to us, and hope becomes alive in our hearts. They speak of the privilege that God's people have in approaching the throne of grace with confidence because of Jesus' atoning work and their adoption and acceptance as children of God (1 John 3:2). The people of God can approach God with freedom and with respectful fear. Holy boldness in prayer encourages us to ask boldly because nothing

---

125 CD_ROM, adapted.
126 For vv. 16 & 17, see my book *Getting to grips with prayer*, chapter 6 (Day One, 2017).
127 Verse 3b of 'What various hindrance we meet'.

is out of bounds. Jesus said, 'According to your faith let it be to you' (Matthew 9:29). Caleb asked (of Joshua), 'Give me this mountain' (Joshua 14:9–15) when 85 years old, but age had not killed the vision or the calling. The word *confidence* (*parresia*, 1 John 5:14; 2:28; 4:17), speaks of boldness and has the idea of lack of shame; it allows frankness, clarity, and an openness which leads to plain speaking without concealment (3:21; Mark 11:24; John 11:14). John uses it three other times in this Epistle, speaking of: freedom from shame (2:28); frankness and openness (3:21) fearlessness at the judgement seat (4:17). Bold *supplication* is the intense, sincere and urgent prayer, of the heart and is full of boldness. It will not take 'no' for an answer. Hannah, wife of Elkanah, was at her wits end when she prayed for a baby (1 Samuel 1:10–11)! Jesus said, 'The kingdom of heaven suffers violence, and the violent takes it by force,' to encourage to pray frankly and earnestly. There are things we will *not* receive unless we *ask earnestly* for them. We know the Father hears us because the cross has opened up communication *and* fellowship with our Father in heaven. Confidence turns to assurance when we walk with God: 'We know that we have the petitions that we have asked of Him' (1 John 5:15b). Prayer, however, is not a device to impose our will on God or to change God's mind in our favour. We see that successful prayer is a confident, holy courage residing in the believer's heart and seen by earnest prayers. 'It is not enough to yield assent to the divine word unless it is accompanied with true and pure affection, so that our hearts are not double or divided' (J. Calvin).[128]

Paul helps us to pray well

Paul was a man whose prayers have been left for us to learn from. He *prayed in the Spirit* and places before us the principal realities of the Christian life. His prayers are very instructive as they flow from his pastoral heart and spiritual mind to successive generations of pastors to learn from,

---

128 John Calvin, *Commentary on 1 John*.

(Ephesians 1:16–19f; Philippians 1:9–11; 2 Thessalonians 1:11–12); they also do more than that as they show us:

1. How the saints are to pray for themselves and each other. A. W. Pink puts it this way, that what the apostles requested in prayer for the saints 'are the particular things which Christians in all ages are to especially desire, prize and seek an increase of'.[129] Thus Paul's requests are for things Christians in all ages are especially to value and ask for.

2. We often pray for earthly things, while Paul prays for spiritual and heavenly things. We usually forget the great spiritual realities while Paul grasps their ultimate importance.

3. He prays to the One who alone can impart such blessings: 'the God of our Lord Jesus Christ, the Father of glory' (Ephesians 1:17). This is a clear rejection of prayer directed to other gods or past saints.

Colossians 1:9–14

In his opening words in praise of the Colossians (vv. 3–8), the apostle tells them that he is praying for them: 'We give thanks to the God and Father of our Lord Jesus Christ, praying always for you', and continues:

We ... do not cease to pray for you, and to ask that you may be filled with the knowledge of His will in all wisdom and spiritual understanding; that you may walk worthy of the Lord, fully pleasing Him, being fruitful in every good work and increasing in the knowledge of God; strengthened with all might, according to His glorious power, for all patience and longsuffering with joy. (vv. 9–11)

---

129 A. W. Pink, *The Prayers of Paul* (Chicago: Moody Press, 1973), p. 222.

The Greek word for 'pray' (*proseuchomai*) speaks of talking to God. It is never used of petitions to men.[130] Prayer is talking face to face with God. He then plainly encourages prayers of thanksgiving by reminding them of their experience of the gospel realities:

Giving thanks to the Father who has qualified us to be partakers of the inheritance of the saints in the light. He has delivered us from the power of darkness and conveyed us into the kingdom of the Son of His love, in whom we have redemption through His blood, the forgiveness of sins. (vv. 12–14)

Paul teaches us *what* to pray

The news that Epaphras brought produced 'an upsurge of prayer'. Paul the man of prayer was committed to the task of intercession: *we do not cease to pray for you*. It is important that pastors and elders in the local churches pray aright, and Paul's prayers teach us to pray well. He shows to pastors what they should pray and that prayer is to be prayer made in the Spirit's strength (Ephesians 6:18), *with the understanding* (1 Corinthians 14:15). In Paul's prayers of intercession we have clearly illustrated the content of prayer. Through these examples the Holy Spirit teaches us *what* to pray (cf. Romans 8:26–27). As we follow the blueprint of Paul's prayers we learn what the substance of our own prayers should be. When Paul prays for them he does not pray alone: note: the *we* passages (vv. 3, 9). He prays for them in the company of others. Paul knew the value of believing intercession motivated by faith and love (cf. 2 Corinthians 1:11). We learn, therefore, that prayer is a very important ministry; prayer meetings are very important gatherings; time spent in prayer is redeeming the time; and those who pray together grow together in grace, joy and hope.

Paul had a prayer list. The material in our prayers is very important. What was it that the Holy Spirit led Paul to request?

---

130 The prefix *pro* 'gives the idea of definiteness and directness in prayer' (Wuset).

'Be filled with the knowledge of His will' (v. 9). The early Gnostic sect loved this word *knowledge*. It was a key word for the spoilers who crept in unawares. However, the apostle prays that they will possess the real (spiritual) thing in Jesus Christ our Saviour, and not in part but in fullness so that there is no room left for self or the world in our hearts.[131] Christians need to know 'what is that good and acceptable and perfect will of God' (Romans 12:1–2), and Paul makes this obvious by his recorded printed prayers.

Wisdom will help us to make a right and good use of knowledge, while *spiritual understanding* is to have discernment. This come from walking in the Spirit and holding a biblical world-view.

Thus, being filled with *knowledge of His will in all wisdom and spiritual understanding* keeps us on the right path. How important it is to know and 'understand what the will of the Lord is' (Ephesians 5:17). When Paul was converted on the Damascus Road he asked the Saviour, 'What must I do?' The under-shepherds of Jesus Christ need to be 'filled with the knowledge of His will in all wisdom and spiritual understanding'. They need what is revealed, 'precept upon precept, line upon line, here a little and there a little.'

The will of God leads us to walk with God in *fruitfulness* (v. 10). Enoch walked with God (Genesis 5:24) and so must pastors if they would be co-workers with Christ (cf. Ephesians 2:10). Their aim should be to please Him not out of duty but out of love and faithful stewardship. 'Being fruitful in every good work' is being a co-worker with God. Prayer has a goal and a target: it requests and longs for fruitfulness, 'fully pleasing Him, being fruitful in every good work'. Walking worthy (holy lives) and fruitfulness go together.

Preachers need to search their hearts and ask what hinders blessing, and make this prayer for themselves constantly. Only in the potential of Christ's power can pastors be faithful to their heavenly calling and be:

---

131 See my book *Opening Up Colossians and Philemon* (Leominster: Day One, 2006).

'Strengthened with all might, according to His glorious power, for all patience and long suffering with joy' (v. 11). Pastors are in continual need of the Lord's *power* (*kratos*) to be strong, and therefore Paul prays for divine supernatural strength. God provides *His* pastors with power to be faithful in His will to the end of the journey.

Paul knows also that perseverance requires patience, longsuffering and joy; these too *must* also be requested in prayer. Two similar words are used here, and possession of these two graces will enable one's joyfulness in ministry and service to continue and remain no matter what. There is something miraculous here, for Paul is praying for the sense of inner *joy* when times are hard and days are evil and he is in prison!

In Colossians 1:12–14 Paul summarises the divine works of redemption. Thus there should be prayers of thankfulness, gladness in our public intercessions for what God has done for us in Christ:

> Giving thanks unto the Father who has qualified us to be partakers of the inheritance of the saints in the light. He has delivered us from the power of darkness and conveyed us into the kingdom of the Son of His love … in whom we have redemption through His blood, the forgiveness of sins.

Thankfulness for our inheritance—*qualifying us to be partakers of the inheritance*—which is 'incorruptible and undefiled … reserved in heaven' for us (1 Peter 1:4), because of our deliverance—being *delivered from the power of darkness and conveyed into the kingdom of the Son of His love* with *the forgiveness of sins*—joy and peace should be evident in public prayers and not only in private worship. For these reasons praise in the public place before God will be welcomed by redeemed souls. Paul is teaching the church in Colosse that:

- Pastors *and* elders ought to pray for the flock that God has charged them to oversee.

- Believers ought to pray for themselves and for each other, for it shows us the big picture and teaches the availability of grace in time of need.

- To be publicly thankful to God who has provided an inheritance through the death and resurrection of Jesus Christ is good.

- What it is to begin to 'pray in the Spirit'.

Thomas Manton and other Puritans see prayer as a duty and as a means of grace. He says when we pray, 'There is not a change in God, but a change in us, wrought by prayer. It is neither to give information to God, that He may know our meaning, nor to move Him and persuade Him to be willing by our much speaking, but only to raise up our own faith and hope towards God.'[132] The Westminster Larger Catechism agrees:

Q.154. *What are the outward means whereby Christ communicates to us the benefits of His mediation?*

Ans. The outward and ordinary means whereby Christ communicates to His church the benefits of His mediation, are all His ordinances; especially the word, sacraments and prayer; all which are made effectual to the elect for their salvation.

The Reformed Baptists agreed: John Bunyan said: 'Prayer is an ordinance of God to be used both in public and private; yea, such an ordinance as brings those that have the spirit of supplication into great familiarity with God.' It is also so prevalent an action that 'it gets from God', both of the person that prayed, and for them that are prayed for, great things.[133] While Benjamin Keach's Baptist Catechism (1677) concurs:

---

132 Thomas Manton, *Daily Readings*, 10 August.
133 John Bunyan, *Prayer*, p.11.

Chapter 12

Q.95. *What are the outward and ordinary means whereby Christ communicates to us the benefits of redemption?*

Ans. The outward and ordinary means whereby Christ communicates to us the benefits of redemption are His ordinances, especially the Word, Baptism, the Lord's Supper and Prayer; all which are made effectual to the elect for salvation.

By prayer, Manton said, we are to come apart with God; we should 'open the matter (issues) to God, [this] is a mighty ease to the soul'.[134] He is saying we are to pray because we need the blessings that result from being in Jesus' presence and sharing communion as Father with child, and says, 'a word from a child moves the father more than an orator can move all his hearers'.[135]

The duty to pray well

Duty being a legal term brings a moral or legal obligation to it by normal definition, including a responsibility; but is it too legalistic to call prayer a *duty*? The word 'duty' is not used very much in the koine Greek of the New Testament (Greek *opheilē*, a debt, i.e. 'what is owing'; and in modern Greek 'a must'). Its use in Romans 15:27, 'they owe it to the Jews' to supply food, etc., and again in 1 Corinthians 7:3, 'what is due to her', i.e. to one's spouse, shows a duty is due. Some Puritans like Manton saw prayer as a personal duty: 'We are to be often with God, and to keep up not only a praying frame, but a constant correspondence with Him', noting that 'Jesus Christ went aside to pray to God: therefore, if we are Christians, so it should so be with us.'[136] For Manton, prayer is:

1. an important and necessary duty: for gospel success and protection;

---

134 Thomas Manton, *Daily Readings*, 6 August.
135 Ibid., 9 August.
136 Ibid., 3 August.

2. a personal duty: in secret alone with God pouring out our heart to Him (Job 16:20);

3. a patient duty: that waits for answers (cf. importunity, which is urgent and pressing);

4. a lonely duty: watching and praying is done in the closet alone with God;

5. a rewarded duty: we get something from God through prayer.

We are by Scripture duty-bound, i.e. obliged and honour-bound, to come to the place of prayer, personally (privately) seeing that there is a duty of repentance; a duty of faith; a duty of joy; and a duty of stewardship. We are called in Scripture to give what we *owe* to God: reverential fear, willing oblation, daily thanksgiving, praise and worship, sincere love in communion with the Father in heaven.

If prayer is also a *duty* then communion in earnest prayer for gospel preachers and evangelists and missionaries and ourselves is called for. All the above duties are placed on the hearts by the Holy Spirit. Is it *too* legalistic to call prayer a duty? If so, it needs to be seen as a duty of love.

Bunyan called prayer 'the opener of the heart of God, and a means by which the soul, though empty, is filled. By prayer the Christian can open his heart to God, as to a friend, and to obtain fresh testimony of God's friendship to him'.[137] Thus in these senses prayer is a privileged duty and a theme that comes through time and time again in Puritan writings because it is seen as a means of grace. For Bunyan, 'Prayer is an ordinance of God ... it gets from God.'[138] Thus, blessings flow from 'sincere, sensible, affectionate pouring out of the heart or souls to God, through Christ, in the strength and assistance of the Holy Spirit'.[139]

---

137 John Bunyan, *Prayer*, p.11.
138 Ibid.
139 Ibid.

13. Praying in the Spirit

'Paul teaches that it is certainly in order to pray with the spirit, so long as the mind, i.e. the understanding, is brought into play. He therefore allows and approves the use of spiritual gifts in prayers; but he insists that the mind should not be inactive, and that of course, is the main point.' (John Calvin)[140]

'Without the special aid and assistance of the Holy Spirit no man knoweth what to pray for as he ought.' (John Owen)[141]

'The great tragedy of life is not unanswered prayer but unoffered prayer.' (F. B. Meyer)

'By prayer and petition with thanksgiving, let your requests be made known to God.' (Philippians 4:6)

'When You said, "Seek My face", My heart said to You, "Your face, Lord, I will seek."' (Psalm 27:8)

Our Saviour wants His under-shepherds to be constant in prayer—and when the spiritual battle is raging elders must persevere with a disciplined approach. This emphasis is made by the New Testament writers; Paul; 'Continue in prayer, and watch in the same with thanksgiving' (Colossians 4:2). Also Peter; 'But the end of all things is at hand; therefore be serious and watchful in your prayers' (1 Peter 4:7).

---

140 John Calvin, *1 Corinthians* (Grand Rapids, MI: Eerdmans Publishing, 1996), p. 292.
141 *Works*, IV. 271.

These two apostles were aware of the spiritual battle for souls against the evil adversary Satan.

Prayer finds its voice where hope is present in the soul while hopeless prayers are wasted prayers. The covenant love and *'exceeding great and precious'* promises of God our Redeemer are incentives to call on the name of Jesus Christ. Faith knows that our Father in heaven is alive, loving and almighty and is always glad to hear prayer for His adopted children (Jeremiah 33:3). This is solid ground for believers when it comes to prayer. All prayer must be made in Jesus Christ's name with faith (John 16:23; Hebrews 11:33; 2 Peter 1:4). God's people are requested to seek in order to find (Luke 11:9–10). This reminds us all that faith and love is more powerful than what is imagined by wickedness as magic.

God loves to hear the prayers of His people, for prayer is God's idea! Thomas Manton (1620–1677) encouraged prayer by saying, 'If we give thanks for so much grace as we have already received, it is the way to increase our store.'[142] John Bunyan defines prayer thus: 'Prayer is a sincere, sensible, affectionate pouring out of the heart or souls to God, through Christ, in the strength and assistance of the Holy Spirit, for such things as God has promised, or according to His Word, for the good of the church, with submission in faith to the will of God.'[143] By this, he makes it clear that Christians must keep praying, claiming the promises of God. God's pastors therefore should be much in prayer showing shameless boldness at the throne of grace (Hebrews 4:16). This calls for committed and believing intercession where there is: *(i)* fellowship in Christ Jesus with the Father aided by the Spirit; *(ii)* reverent and respectful entreaty with repentance; *(iii)* duty prayers for gospel success and protection; *(iv)* offerings of love and oblation. Praying well is not achieved without the help of the Spirit of God; just as worship requires 'Spirit and truth' (John 4:24), so prayer requires the guidance of the Holy Spirit (Romans 8:26). The Spirit is a

---

142 Ibid., 19 August.
143 John Bunyan, *Prayer* (London: The Banner of Truth Trust, 1965), p. 13.

Spirit of supplications; as Ferguson notes, 'He is not formally the one who makes supplication but He works in and through the believers prayers, creating a gracious inclination to the duty of prayer, and giving a similarly gracious inclination to discharge it.' [144] This was emphasised by the British Puritans and also by Bunyan who said, 'the Spirit by the Word directs in the manner as well as the matter of prayer', and is 'the helper and governor of the soul when it prays according to the will of God; so it [sic] guides by and according to the Word of God and His promises'.[145]

The Holy Spirit in Puritan thought

The Puritans believed that Christians could not pray successfully without the aid of the Holy Spirit. R. Hollingworth, says: 'The work of the Holy Spirit in prayer [is] in regard to the person: enlightening; enlivening; enlarging; in regard to the prayer: exciting; discovering; bringing to our remembrance the savoury and suitable passages of holy Writ, especially the precious promises [and] exciting graces of prayer: the enlarging of our affections "with sighs and groans" [and the] restraining our tongue".[146] The Spirit's ministry is vital to enable right prayer. Richard Baxter believes: 'True Christian prayer is the believing or serious expressing or acting of our lawful desires before God, through Jesus our Mediator, by the help of the Holy Spirit, as means to procure of Him the grant of these desires'.[147] While William Gurnall says: 'To pray in faith is to ask of God, in the name of Christ, what He hath promised, relying on His power and truth for performance, without binding Him up to time, manner or means.' [148] The Puritans do not despise the human understanding.

---

144 S. B. Ferguson, *John Owen on the Christian Life* (Edinburgh: The Banner of Truth Trust, 1995), p. 227.
145 John Bunyan, ibid., pp. 23ff.
146 R. Hollingworth, *The Holy Ghost on the Bench*, chapter V. Quoted in Nuttall, *The Holy Spirit in Puritan Faith and Experience*, p. 65.
147 Richard Baxter, *A Christian Directory*, p. 483.
148 W. Gurnall, *The Christian in Complete Armour* (Edinburgh: The Banner of Truth Trust, 1995), Vol. 2, p. 338.

The first thing to notice about prayer is that prayer in the Spirit is essential to communion with the Father. G. F. Nuttall 'regards the principle of prayer as a familiar communion with the Father'.[149] However, John Owen 'does not think the Spirit inspires our supplications by an immediate divine revelation as He inspired the Prophets of old, but rather by giving voice and action to—indeed making actual—our desires and requests'.[150] Sinclair B. Ferguson, in *John Owen on the Christian Life*, says, for 'Owen prayer is regarded as inseparable from our experience of God, for prayer is "a gracious work"'. The Holy Spirit works in our wills and affections enabling us to have a sense of the value of the Christian's needs. He gives a 'delight in God' as the 'object of prayer'. For prayer 'is a covenant privilege, and draws its inspiration, both in content and manner, from what the Christian learns of God as the God of promise in the covenant, and through the Holy Spirit.'[151]

Secondly: the Holy Spirit is a guide and a help to the substance or matter of prayer. John Owen recognised a distinct 'gift' of prayer. The Holy Spirit is a Spirit of supplications: 'He is not formally the one who makes supplication but he works in and through the believers' prayers, creating a gracious inclination to the duty of prayer, and giving a similarly gracious inclination to discharge it. Owen sees both aspects included in the statement of Romans (8.26)'.[152] The problem of the dual intercession of both the ascended Jesus Christ and the Holy Spirit in Romans 8:26,34, where Christ is said to live to make intercession and the Spirit Himself also 'makes intercession for us', is handled by Owen in his expounding of Zechariah 12:10.[153] Wakefield also helpfully writes: 'The Holy Spirit cannot make intercession to Himself or He would be less than God; nor can He interpose in heaven on our behalf, for that is the priestly office

---

149 G. F. Nuttall, *The Holy Spirit in Puritan Faith and Experience*, p. 66.
150 G. S. Wakefield, *Puritan Devotion* (London: Epworth Press, 1957), pp. 81–82.
151 S. B. Ferguson, *John Owen on the Christian Life*, p. 228.
152 S. B. Ferguson, *John Owen on the Christian Life*, p. 227.
153 J. Owen, *Works*, IV, 254ff

of Christ. His intercessions is—using the scholastic term of Owen—"efficient"; that is, He works in us, stirring us up to pray, and He makes us able to pray. Thus it is by the strength and assistance of the Holy Spirit that we are enabled, albeit groaningly, to approach God through Christ. He is the Spirit of Christ, the legacy of the Lord now in Glory, [and our hearts turn] to Him who pleads before the throne.'[154] Sinclair Ferguson notes that in Owen's thinking, we as sinners lack conviction so, 'God the Holy Spirit brings us to our sense of depravity, awareness of need and to the confession of our creaturely ignorance.'[155] John Bunyan writes: 'We know not the matter of the things for which we should pray ... what man of his own brain may imagine and devise, is one thing, and what they are commanded, and ought to do, is another."[156]

Thirdly: the Holy Spirit inspires confidence in prayer. G. F. Nuttall said that there is a close connection 'between the "witness of the Spirit" and "the Spirit and prayer". It is in prayer, pre-eminently, that we see, talking effect, the God-ward aspect of the Spirit's witness. That witness is "that we are the children of God" and this means, that towards God we may behave with the freedom and fervent familiarity of His children.'[157] Owen teaches there is also in prayer, 'a confidence of acceptance ... that is, that God is well pleased with their duties, accepting both them and their persons in Christ. Without this we can have no delight in prayer or in God as the object of it'.[158] Bunyan believed that 'it is the Spirit only that can teach us to ask; it (sic) only being able to search out all things ... without which Spirit, though we had a thousand Common Prayer Books, yet we know not what we should pray for as we ought".[159] R. Sibbes (1577–1635) speaking on the spirit on adoption thinks 'that "Abba, Father", it is a bold

---

154 G. S. Wakefield, *Puritan Devotion*, p. 80.
155 S. B. Ferguson, *John Owen on the Christian Life*, p. 226.
156 John Bunyan, *Prayer*, p. 25.
157 G. F. Nuttall, *The Holy Spirit in Puritan Faith and Experience*, pp. 62–63.
158 J. Owen, *Works*, IV., 294.
159 John Bunyan, *Prayer*, pp. 24–25.

and familiar speech … there is an inward kind of familiar boldness in the soul, whereby a Christian goes to God, as a child when he wants anything goes to his father. A child considers not his own worthiness or means, but goeth to his father familiarly and boldly. This comes from the Spirit. If we be sons, then we have the Spirit, whereby we cry Abba, Father'.[160] 'Prayer is not only an exercise of grace, but a response to our relationship and standing with God the Father as His adopted children.'[161] The simple cry of the child is true prayer. Owen declares: 'There is no more required unto prayer either way but our crying, "Abba, Father"'.[162]

Fourthly: stinted forms of praying were frowned upon. Horton Davies lays out five reasons why the Puritan's rejected 'stinted forms' of praying:

(*i*) John Owen reckoned that set forms of prayer deprived both the minister and people the gift of prayer saying 'we daily see men napkining (sic) their talents until they are taken from them'.[163] Thus 'set forms of prayer hinder the progress of the individual in the gift and grace of prayer'.

(*ii*) 'They could not meet the varied needs of differing congregations and occasions. While the Book of Common Prayer was comprehensive in its appeal, it lacked the particularity and intimacy of free prayer.'

(*iii*) 'Because they were regularly prescribed they persuaded the people that they were necessary and that God could not be worshiped in any other way'. John Owen 'regarded their very uniformity as a danger' and reckoned that as they appear to be indispensable they were put on a par with Scripture itself. Baxter said that 'congregations must not overvalue set forms as necessities of worship'; .

(*iv*) 'They conduced to hypocrisy.' Either familiarity breeds contempt or it stimulates an attitude which is not really felt. It produces mere lip service.

---

160 R. Sibbes, *Works*, III.456f.; IV.232f., quoted in Nuttall, ibid., p.64.
161 Quoted in S.B. Ferguson, *John Owen on the Christian Life*, p.228.
162 Quoted, G.S. Wakefield, *Puritan Devotion*, p.81, see Owen's *Works*, IV. 269.
163 *napkining*, Old English; implies covering up of their God-given gifts.

(v) 'The final charge against set prayers is that their imposition has brought persecution.' John Owen accused the imposers of liturgies of bringing "fire and faggot into the Christian religion"'.[164]

The Prayer Book

Bunyan's rejection of the Prayer Book was symptomatic of the Puritan and Independent attitude after the Ejection of 1662.[165] Wakefield said Bunyan considered that 'the Prayer Book is virtually forbidden in Scripture by all the prohibitions of feasts and new moons and vain repetitions. Even the Lord's Prayer can become blasphemy if uttered without Spirit or understanding'.[166] It was never intended, he believed, as a 'stinted form' but as a model of prayer. Approaching the Almighty must not be undertaken flippantly or without faith, it must be 'sensible'. That is, it must have knowledge, and be conscious of the danger of sin, the mercy of God and the willingness of God to give mercy. This will encourage us to pray for cleansing in the blood of Christ.

Prayer must be 'through Christ' says Bunyan 'or else it must be questioned, whether it is prayer', and he adds: 'This coming to God through Christ is the hardest part of prayer. Here the mystery of grace is perceived for to come through Christ is for the sinner to be enabled of God to hide himself under the shadow of the Lord Jesus as a man hides under a thing for safety. Through Christ we find favour with God, so faith is essential as by it we put on Christ and in Him appear before God. So when we pray we must come to God by Christ's merits, in His blood, righteousness, victory, intercession and so stand before Him, being "accepted in the beloved"'.[167] Gurnall makes the same plea, he too wants us to pray in Christ's name: 'As there can be no faith but on a promise, so

---

164 Horton Davies, *The Worship of the English Puritans* (Morgan, PA: Solo Deo Gloria Publications, 1997), pp. 103–109.
165 Ibid, p. 101.
166 G. S. Wakefield, *Puritan Devotion* (London: Epworth Press, 1957), p. 69.
167 John Bunyan, *Prayer*, p. 19.

no promise can be claimed but in His name.' He continues: 'The promise of eternal life was made to Christ "before the world began"; we come to our right in the promise as co-heirs with Christ. He shed His blood and now, God acknowledges the debt to Christ and bound Himself to perform. So we must plead 'under the protection of His name.'[168]

As to whether our private prayers are true before God Bunyan believed, like most Puritans, that 'prayer is only true when it is within the compass of God's Word; it is blasphemy, or at best vain babbling, when the petition is unrelated to the Book'.[169] This is a very important factor when it comes to what Puritans believed about prayer. It is not only a constantly recurring theme but one that is stressed most emphatically. Gurnall makes the same emphasis saying: 'We must ask what God has promised, or we choose ourselves and not beg; we subject God's will to ours, and not ours to His; we forge bond and claim it as a debt, which is a horrible presumption. He that is his own promiser must be his own paymaster.'[170] John Owen, too, believed the content of prayer should be held within scriptural grounds. The theology of this goes back, at least, as far as Tertullian who distinguished between 'legitimate' and 'illegitimate' prayer. For Owen, Scripture dictated the content and inspired the activity of prayer.[171] Puritans advise believers to keep their eye on the Word of God when they pray.

Bunyan endorsed the Puritans' view that Christians cannot pray successfully without the aid of the Spirit. Prayer must be 'by the strength or assistance of the Spirit'. It is the Holy Spirit who quickens and stirs the heart, 'by, with and through the Word, by bringing that to the heart'. 'The Spirit by the Word directs in the manner as well as the matter of prayer',

168 W. Gurnall, *The Christian in Complete Armour* (Edinburgh: The Banner of Truth Trust, 1995), Vol. 2, pp. 338–339.

169 John Bunyan, *Prayer*, p. 20.

170 W. Gurnall, *The Christian in Complete Armour*, Vol. 2, p. 338.

171 S. B. Ferguson, *John Owen on the Christian Life* (Edinburgh: The Banner of Truth Trust, 1987), p. 229.

and is 'the helper and governor of the soul when it prays according to the will of God; so it (sic) guides by and according to the Word of God and His promises'. What is it to pray with the Spirit? Bunyan is sure: 'The prayer that goes to heaven is the one that is sent thither in the strength of the Spirit.' As to the content of our personal prayers Bunyan says prayer is to be made for the good of the church, i.e. for the honour of God, for Christ's advancement and for the people's benefit. If you 'pray for the peace of Jerusalem, you pray for all that is required of you'. All prayer must be clothed in humility as a result; prayer submits to the will of God. Let God dispose of our prayers as 'his heavenly wisdom sees fit'.[172]

Watch and pray

Our Lord in His time of severest trial encouraged His disciples to *watch and pray* (Mark 14:38) and was conscious of His ministry of prayer to Peter and the others (Luke 22:31–32). Spurgeon stressed the necessity of intercession of the churches: 'I must myself mount the watch-tower, and watch unto prayer. Our heavenly Protector foresees all the attacks which are about to be made upon us, and when as yet the evil designed [for] us is but in the desire of Satan, Jesus prays for us that our faith fail not, when we are sifted as wheat. Continue O gracious Watchman, to forewarn us of our foes, and for Zion's sake hold not thy peace.'[173] 'Watch and pray': what can it mean? I suggest:

'WATCH' *WHEN* YOU PRAY

Regular and planned times using a prayer list are always best. We must also be open to those times when Jesus may be found (in times of revival when the spiritual battle is at its strongest and when the sensible presence of the Holy Spirit is discerned). Opportunity demands action. Jesus asked the disciples with Him in Gethsemane to *watch and pray*. There He was,

---

172 John Bunyan, *Prayer*, p. 22.
173 C. H. Spurgeon, *Morning & Evening*, August 6; adapted.

personally praying in agony and *they* were sleeping. They had not yet learned what the spiritual battle was about or how to cope with it and win through. There are times in our life when more prayer and not less is required. The Saviour's words are relevant for us still: 'Watch and pray, lest you enter into temptation. The spirit indeed is willing, but the flesh is weak.' 'What! Could you not watch with Me one hour?' However, their opportunity to pray with Jesus was gone! (Matthew 26:40).

'WATCH' FOR *OPPORTUNITIES* TO PRAY

Zeal and love alert us to be awake and watching. Providences and opportunities are important here. The men of Issachar understood the times in which they lived, so we must not be ignorant about what to pray for in our day (1 Chronicles 12:32). The parable of the Friend at Midnight teaches that circumstances can come along that give us an opportunity to pray well (Luke 11:5–13). Jesus' concluding words (v. 13) may imply that only with the aid of the Holy Spirit can that be done well. In John 17 before Jesus' passion He prayed the greatest prayer the world has heard, ever: 'Father … I have glorified You on the earth. I have finished the work which You have given Me to do' (v. 4). In His sufferings our Saviour opened His heart to the Father willingly with oblation and hope. Prayer is the cry of a burdened heart with its fondness, but it requires faith and hope also. Thus our zeal must be according to knowledge. Bible truth and Bible promises must be kept before us in order to pray well. It helps to ask 'in Jesus' name' (John 15:16) and to seek the help of the Holy Spirit (Romans 8:26f). Let us remember that God the Almighty is not our servant to do our bidding when we please, but a loving Father in heaven who willingly hears the prayers of His people. Let us remember also the devil sometimes tells us it is useless to pray, especially when it is important to do so urgently! 'Satan', said Samuel Chadwick, 'dreads nothing but prayer, his one concern is to keep the saint from praying. He fears nothing from fearless study, prayer-less work and prayer-less religion. He laughs at our toil, mocks our wisdom, but trembles when we pray'.[174]

'WATCH' OUT FOR *WHAT* STOPS YOU PRAYING

Personal sin will dull your spirit and hinder prayer. Unbelief will grieve the Spirit and prayer will be an absent activity as a result. Worldliness will put prayer not only to bed but to sleep! In his book *The Pilgrim's Progress* John Bunyan wrote about the *Enchanted Ground* which kept many professors of religion from heaven. This dangerous state was to be avoided at all costs when one is on one's way to the *Celestial City*: '"What is to be done", asked Christian, "to ensure wakefulness when crossing the Enchanted Ground"?, Hopeful his companion replied, "one of the best plans is to keep Christian fellowship and talk about the ways of the Lord."'[175] If we grieve the Spirit the blessings of Christian fellowship and 'praying well' are lost (Ephesians 4:30–32).

'WATCH' FOR *ANSWERS* TO YOUR PRAYERS

This will draw out praise and brings joy to the soul. Let us continue consistently in prayer that answers to His promises will be known. Paul exhorts the Colossian congregation to *'continue earnestly in prayer, being vigilant in it with thanksgiving'* (4:2). Pastors and members must remember that spiritual lethargy is like a virus which affects all of church life. Similarly, the virus of prayerlessness limits prayer to selfish requests, to the neglect of the greater spiritual realities. Chadwick said, 'There is always the sweat of blood in prevailing intercession'[176], hence the need for 'continuing steadfastly in prayer' (Romans 12:12). The Greek verb form translated 'continuing steadfastly' (*proskartereō*) can be translated as 'I persist'. The same verb is used in Acts 1:14, and can be translate as,

---

174 Samuel Chadwick, *The Path of Prayer* (London: Hodder & Stoughton, 1968), p.81.

175 An extract from C.H.Spurgeon, *Pictures from Pilgrim's Progress* (London: Passmore and Alabaster, 1903).

176 Samuel Chadwick, *The Path of Prayer*, p.81.

'continually devoting'. The call to dedication in the work of prayer is not a call to a monastic life, but rather to be in the world (but not *of* the world), remembering that 'where prayer is prevailing the kingdom of God has prospered, where prayer is lukewarm it is languishing'.[177]

177 J. Oswald Sanders, *Effective Prayer* (London: OMF, 1972), p. 5.

14. Spiritual warfare

'Indeed, to preach the word of God is nothing less than to bring upon oneself all the furies of hell and of Satan, and therefore also of … every power of the world. It is the most dangerous kind of life to throw oneself in the way of Satan's many teeth.' (Martin Luther) [178]

'Didst thou never learn to outshoot the devil with his own bow, and to cut off his own head with his own sword, as David served Goliath? If you get this art so as to out run him in his own shoes and to make his own darts to pierce himself then you can say, now do Satan's temptations, as well as all other things, work together for my good.' (G. B. Cheever) [179]

Pastors 'are the spiritual eyes of the community. They keep open the highway to heaven and constantly call all to take that route. At the same time they warn about the broad road that leads to everlasting hell. For these reasons pastors suffer opposition and satanic attack. Of this we can be sure, a faithful godly pastor is one in a thousand (Job 33:23).' (Erroll Hulse) [180]

'The God of peace will crush Satan under your feet shortly.' (Romans 16:20)

---

178 Martin Luther, 'On the Councils and the Church', in Martin Luther's *Basic Theological Writings* (*Weimarer Ausgabe*), 25: 253.
179 G. B. Cheever, 'Satan's Temptations', in *'The Christian Treasury': Contributions from Ministers and Members* (Edinburgh: John Johnstone, 1846), p. 247.
180 Erroll Hulse, 'What is a Pastor?', *Reformation Today*, No. 249, 2012 (Sept–Oct), p. 9.

In Psalm 62 we see King David (the shepherd of his people) trusting God at all times:

> My soul, wait silently for God alone, for my expectation is from Him. He only is my rock and my salvation; He is my defence; I shall not be moved. In God is my salvation and my glory; the rock of my strength, and my refuge, is in God. Trust in Him at all times, you people; pour out your heart before Him; God is a refuge for us. *Selah.* (Psalm 62:5–8)

To trust in Jesus Christ *at all times* must replace doing so *some times* or *most times* for *at all times* is the only way forward if the man of God is to fulfil his vocation. Trusting God is the walk of faith, the way of faith and the work of faith. God says to him, 'Trust me', because it will not be long before a new under-shepherd finds himself needing to do so! Trusting in the God of hope is a lifelong exercise: the pastor/under-shepherd must let his public ministry excel so as to glorify his Father in heaven (Matthew 5:16). This is especially so when Christian foundations are being destroyed. He must be 'salt and light' (Matthew 5:13–14) in order to bear witness to God's salvation and Christ's gospel. In a word: he is to do what God has saved and called him to do, and to do it heartily as to the Lord and not to men (Colossians 3:23). There must be reliance on the resurrected and ascended Jesus Christ our High Priest in heaven. Beneficially He watches over His people in times of testing while His love is unfailing every morning.

Holy war

In spiritual warfare three things are pertinent:

FIRSTLY, BE UNTROUBLED

If we are self-sufficient we are inclined to trust in no one but ourselves because we look to our own resources and education. Some trust money.

Yet others rely on family. However, those who trust in Christ depend on the Saviour alone for protection and strength, encouragement and inner peace:

Therefore we do not lose heart. Even though our outward man is perishing, yet the inward man is being renewed day by day. For our light affliction, which is but for a moment, is working for us a far more exceeding and eternal weight of glory, while we do not look at the things which are seen, but at the things which are not seen. For the things which are seen are temporary, but the things which are not seen are eternal. (2 Corinthians 4:16–18)

In the Christian ministry pastors are dependent on the Holy Spirit for help and for assurance that Christ will supply all their needs (Philippians 4:19; 1 Peter 1:5). The Christian life is one of *total dependence* on Christ Jesus. Prayer is of vital importance and it must also be *normal*. Thus pastors should pray daily and 'without ceasing' (Ephesians 6:18; 1 Thessalonians 5:17). We cannot keep ourselves secure, but the Bible makes it clear that 'our sufficiency is from God' (2 Corinthians 3:5). Confidence in Christ Himself is essential if we are to bear fruit. Are we confident that our Saviour is able to keep us from falling (Jude 24)? If so, what does that require on our part? Remember, trusting someone entails the conviction that they can be fully depended upon; so their character and their motives are of vital importance. We must take into account their integrity of character and their ability to give the help required. These vital qualities are found in Jesus Christ our Saviour (1 John 4:8,10; Philippians 1:6; cf. Jeremiah 29:11–12). Exercising faith in Him will place our future in His hands. It has been noted that God is our Trustee and He has promised to manage all our affairs and to manage them well. Thus if we deal with God it must be on the basis of a confidence that holds fast. We face many problems in life and there are times when we do not know what to do or where to turn. These are further opportunities to fully trust our Saviour's love and His promises to us (Psalm 32:10; Proverbs 3:5–6; Matthew 6:5–15; 2 Corinthians 5:7).

SECONDLY, BE PATIENT

My soul, wait silently for God alone, for my expectation is from Him. He only is my rock and my salvation; He is my defence; I shall not be moved. In God is my salvation and my glory; the rock of my strength, and my refuge, is in God. Trust in Him at all times, you people; pour out your heart before Him; God is a refuge for us. Selah (Psalm 62:5–8)

Trust without patience is putting 'self' on the throne; however, exercising patience is letting Christ sit on the throne of our hearts. If we really trust Christ we will triumph over our impatience. King David found patience: 'My soul, wait silently for God alone, for my expectation is from Him.' (Psalm 62:5). There is need for us to be patient (Psalm 123:1–2; Hebrews 10:35–36). Patience is not procrastination (delaying) but flows from a living faith in process (Hebrews 10:36; 11:13–16). It is good to remember that God can answer our prayers in three ways, i.e. yes, no and wait! (1 John 3:22; 5:14). The Christian is called to exercise the grace of patience while awaiting the call to come home to heaven. Patience is the fruit of the Holy Spirit and is a friend to self-control. Trials and problems weary the servant of God, but grace in time of need sustains and provides. James says: 'My brethren, take the prophets, who spoke in the name of the Lord, as an example of suffering and patience. Indeed we count them blessed who endure. You have heard of the perseverance of Job and seen the end intended by the Lord—that the Lord is very compassionate and merciful' (5:10–11) and he uses the Greek word 'endurance', here.[181] The apostle Paul is also clear that this gift is necessary in the work of the ministry: 'Truly the signs of an apostle were accomplished among you with all perseverance' (2 Corinthians 12:12).

---

181 Greek *hupomone*, 'steadfast, consistency, endurance'. A man 'unswerving from his purpose'. 'Loyalty to faith even in times of trial'. Also, 'patient and steadfast' (Thayer, *Lexicon*, p. 644).

THIRDLY, BE HOPEFUL

For we were saved in this hope, but hope that is seen is not hope; for why does one still hope for what he sees? But if we hope for what we do not see, we eagerly wait for it with perseverance. (Romans 8:24–25)

The gift of hope is important to all who would walk in faith and trust with Christ Jesus. Hope is faith together with patience: 'If we hope for what we do not see, we eagerly wait for it with perseverance.' Hope is always about tomorrow. It is not a 'perhaps' or a 'maybe', but a certainty; 'for hope that is seen is not hope' (ibid.). It is 'set before us' in the gospel (Hebrews 6:18) to believe, receive and rely on. The object of hope is God Himself. As the people of God exercise faith in God who is unchangeable, hope settles in their hearts (Hebrews 6:16–17). Hope is always among the people of God because all the promises of God in Christ are 'yes and amen' (2 Corinthians 1:20). We find hope in Hebrews: 'This hope we have as an anchor of the soul, both sure and steadfast' (6:19). Isn't that wonderful? This is why in the Epistle to the Romans, chapter 15, verse 13, Paul calls God 'the God of hope' because 'He remains faithful' (2 Timothy 2:13). It is breathtaking to grasp that our Father in heaven has a plan for each of us. His sovereignty over us is to be cherished and rejoiced in. Let us believe that 'all things work together for good to those who love God, to those who are the called according to His purpose', knowing that after we have suffered for a while His people will be made perfect, be established (in faith), be strengthened (by the Holy Spirit) and be settled (in heart) as to His will for them (Romans 8:28; 1 Peter 5:10). The believer's hope is a 'strong consolation' or, as the NIV puts it, 'a great encouragement' to perseverance. Christian hope is meant to comfort and encourage the downcast. Why does hope comfort and encourage us? Because it is grounded on God's faithfulness and on the trustworthiness of His inspired Word. Because it is 'impossible for God to lie' (Hebrews 6:18). Hope is trust in the 'God of hope' and without hope there is temptation to doubt and impatience is encouraged. However, hope thinks positively and trustingly. The pastor must place his full and unreserved confidence in Christ. He must be dependent on the ascended Saviour for everything required to finish the race (Hebrews 12:1–2). Matthew Henry said: 'All that deal with God must deal upon trust, and He will give comfort to those only that give credit to Him.' [182] Pastors must keep praying and claiming the promises of God with an open Bible in their hands. In times like these pastors should be much in prayer, showing shameless boldness at the throne of grace (Hebrews 4:16).

Conclusion

Pastors are to be prepared for this battle, realise the nature of the battle and recognise the persistency of the battle, remembering also the equipment provided for the battle, viz. *the whole armour of God*. The battle is in the spiritual realm. It is the struggle with Satan, but our victory is assured in Christ when we put on the panoply of God.

Spiritual strength is needed to serve in the pastorate as a calling. It is rigorous and personal and public in its design, so the man of God who answers this call and enters this vocation will need to look to the Holy Spirit for spiritual and physical strength so as to 'run the race with patience' and finish the course. Spurgeon is quite forthright about this and in his clear-cut way counsels that such failure to labour in the strength of the Lord is the preacher's own fault and not His. He wrote:

Want you the bread of life? It drops like manna from the sky. Want you refreshing streams? The rock follows you, and that Rock is Christ. If you suffer any want it is your own fault; if you are straitened you are not straitened in Him, but in your own bowels.[183]

---

182 Matthew Henry, *Commentary*.
183 C.H. Spurgeon, *Morning & Evening*, 24 November.

Pastors need often to come apart and rest in the communion of Christ while using all the private and public means of grace to be strong in the Lord and the power of His might (cf. James 4:7–8a). When it comes to our spiritual encounters with Satan, Jesus has gone before us:

Jesus has *conquered every foe* that obstructs the way. Cheer up now thou faint-hearted warrior. Not only has Christ travelled the road, but He has slain thine enemies:

- Dost thou dread sin? He has nailed it to His cross.

- Dost thou fear death? He has been the death of Death.

- Art thou afraid of hell? He has barred it against the advent of any of His children; they shall never see the gulf of perdition.

- Whatever foes may be before the Christian, they are all overcome.

- There are lions, but their teeth are broken.

- There are serpents, but their fangs are extracted.

- There are rivers, but they are bridged or fordable.

- There are flames, but we wear that matchless garment which renders us invulnerable to fire.

- The sword that has been forged against us is already blunted; the instruments of war which the enemy is preparing have already lost their point.

God has taken away in the person of Christ all the power that Satan and his cohorts can have to hurt us (Colossians 2:15). Thus Spurgeon adds,

'They are beaten, they are vanquished; all you have to do is to divide the spoil. You shall, it is true, often engage in combat; but your fight shall be with a vanquished foe. His head is broken; he may attempt to injure you, but his strength shall not be sufficient for his malicious design. Your victory shall be easy, and your treasure shall be beyond all count.'[184] Hope calls for committed and believing intercession, knowing that 'whatever you ask in My name, that I will do, that the Father may be glorified in the Son. If you ask anything in My name, I will do it' (John 14:13–14). Spurgeon is practical about this:

'All the **strength supplied** to us by our gracious God is meant for service. He said to Peter, "Feed My sheep"; further adding, "Follow Me." Even thus it is with us; we eat the bread of heaven, that we may expend our strength in the Master's service. [As under-shepherds] with staff in hand we come to the Passover, and eat of the paschal lamb with loins girt living *for* Christ and sitting down at the table of our Lord. Serve Him day and night in His temple there eat of heavenly food and render perfect service. Gain strength from Christ to labour for Him by learning how our Lord gives us His grace each day. Daily the Lord feeds and refreshes our souls that we may use our renewed strength in the promotion of His glory.'[185]

Soldiers of Christ, arise,
　And put your armour on,
Strong in the strength which God supplies,
　Through His eternal Son;
Strong in the Lord of Hosts
　And in His mighty pow'r,
Who in the strength of Jesus trusts
　Is more than conqueror.

(Charles Wesley)

---

184 C. H. Spurgeon, *Morning & Evening*, 24 August, adapted.
185 C. H. Spurgeon, *Morning, & Evening*, October 5; adapted.

15. True spirituality

'To be truly Protestant they must be truly Christian.'
(Cornelius Van Til) [186]

'As the people of God we must have faith, for this is the foundation; we must have holiness of life, for this is the superstructure.' (C. H. Spurgeon) [187]

'Joy in God is the most blessed thing of all. This is the third heaven of the believer's privileges—a joy which all the redeemed and sharing with the angels—a joy begun in this world, made perfect in glory.' (Robert Murray M'Cheyne) [188]

The prayer which opens heaven and brings down the Spirit, is not that feeble desire which ceases if it encounters delay or trial of your patience, but that desire that will not go without answer.' (Asahel Nettleton)

The personal practical holiness in pastors and church leaders is an indispensable qualification in the calling of God. Recent exposures in 2021/2 (and before) of pastors and evangelical leaders who have fallen into gross sexual sin and deceit which injured and discredited local churches and agencies questions the truth of the *new*

186 Cornelius Van Til, *The Reformed Pastor & Modern Thought* (Phillipsburg, NJ: Presbyterian and Reformed Pub. Co., 1971), p. 196.
187 C. H. Spurgeon, *Morning & Evening*, 18 September.
188 Robert Murray M'Cheyne, *God Makes A Path*, p. 158.

birth and its power to save and sanctify. The free and powerful grace of God in the redeemed soul is a doctrine held in reformed Protestantism.

The importance of the new birth

God has made us for Himself and it is our destiny in Christ to know Him. It is therefore needful for us to recognise that in Christ we are His children by the new birth through faith or as the apostle John loves to say we are *born of God*:

Little children, let no one deceive you. He who practises righteousness is righteous, just as He is righteous. (1 John 3:7)

Whoever has been born of God does not sin, for His seed remains in him; and he cannot sin, because he has been born of God. (1 John 3:9)

This miracle of regeneration not only secures our justification by faith alone but also our sanctification which ushers in a *true* desire to know and serve God. The believing pastor should serve righteousness just as he served sin before trusting Christ: 'And having been set free from sin, you became slaves of righteousness' (Romans 6:18), i.e. pastors should dedicate their bodies as slaves of righteousness, so that their lives will be truly a holy testimony to their flock and the world (Romans 12:1–2). True spirituality begins with the new birth. There is no side-stepping this truth. There is only one way to God and that is by Jesus Christ who is 'the Door', and the new birth is the key which opens and enters. Those born of God have:

(i) A DESIRE FOR HAPPINESS

'We know', says John, 'that whoever is born of God does not sin' (cf. 3:9). The expression 'does not sin' suggests happiness, to me! If the believer '*does not sin*', that is happiness! Yes? The Greek verb is in the present tense and that means John is speaking of a series of acts or of continuous activity. So he speaks here of habitual sin. He is therefore saying that habitual sin is incompatible with a life of sustained practical righteousness and joy. These spiritual realities will not be absolute until we are 'all changed—in a moment, in the twinkling of an eye, at the last trumpet' (1 Corinthians 15:52). Only death will bring us final victory over the 'old man' and 'original sin'. While the Christian remains on earth he strives to stay clear of sin and sinful attitudes and behaviour; however, indwelling sin remains until heaven is reached, as Paul expressed it: 'For the good that I will to do, I do not do; but the evil I will not to do, that I practise' (Romans 7:19). Because the servant of God will grieve over personal indwelling sin and longs to have the full victory over it in Christ he mourns when it break the sense of fellowship with his Saviour. As a consequence there will be ongoing repentance and faith in the atoning blood of the Lamb of God (1 John 2:1–2). When conviction of sin is known there will be godly sorrow and faith calling him to seek cleansing and peace (2 Corinthians 7:1,10). Such a man of God finds experimental peace when he does those things that are 'pleasing to Him' (2 Corinthians 5:9; Colossians 1:10). Can you see what I am saying? The Christian man, born of God, no longer wants to sin, yet before his conversion that did not trouble him (unless the Spirit was convicting his conscience pre-conversion); now in Christ he is glad when he *feels* that he is walking in sanctified fellowship with his loving Saviour. He has a desire for sanctified happiness born of the indwelling Holy Spirit (Ephesians 4:30).

(ii) A DAWNING OF HOPEFULNESS

'And the wicked one does not touch him' (1 John 5:18). The words, 'touch him' in our text are from the Greek word *haptō* and mean 'to lay hold of' (cf. John 20:17). Here they speak of the assaults of the devil who attacks in order to sever our union with Christ; but he does not 'lay hold of' us because the redeemed are safe in the grace of God which is able to keep them from falling (Jude 24). So there is a dawning of hopefulness for those *born of God* that 'the wicked one does not touch him', i.e. 'lay hold of' him. Persevering security is given to all in Christ. What is promised is as in the Saviour's prayers for us (Luke 22:31), and what blessing is known as we travel to the celestial city of God trusting in the shed blood of the Lamb and looking to the Holy Spirit to guide us (John 16:13); what safeguarding, because 'the wicked one does not touch him'; tempt, yes!; attack, yes!; but he cannot destroy those in Christ in heavenly places (Ephesians 1:3–4f). Pastors are responsible to stay the course; there is no turning back because God promises grace to His adopted children in Christ and they are therefore responsible to persevere in the faith with practical and visible holiness benefiting the local church (2 Corinthians 5:17). Pastors will find as they read and expound the Scriptures that they are safe in Christ their Saviour and they will be able to convey that to their flock when dealing with the doctrine of perseverance.

Here then we see true spirituality's fruits: *(i)* a desire for happiness, and *(ii)* a dawning of hopefulness. These are evidences and the fruits of fellowship with the living God in Christ Jesus and marks of believing perseverance encouraged by the Spirit (Romans 12:12). However, they are to be accompanied by personal righteousness to be reckoned as real and holy and true to the gospel.

The importance of personal righteousness

When the apostle Peter quoted the Old Testament, 'Be holy, for I am holy' (1 Peter 1:16; Leviticus 11:44) he inextricably connected discipleship to a way of life that is both righteous and God glorifying. The New Testament teaches holy living and good works. Such grace bears testimony to the new life received in Christ Jesus and the new mind-set given by Christ's Spirit to all who have believed the gospel unto salvation. Thus, when evil is called good, and good and holy things (and holy people) are called evil, as things are today (especially) in the West, the righteous are called to continue to 'walk as children of light ... walk circumspectly ... redeeming the time, because the days are evil' (Ephesians 5:8–21). As Christians, we are to love our enemies and to subdue personal sin in the strength of the Holy Spirit, bearing witness to the power of the resurrection in our lives. For J.C.Ryle Christian piety is not negotiable: 'There are three things which, according to the Bible, are absolutely necessary to the salvation of every man and woman in Christendom. These three are justification, regeneration and sanctification. All three meet in every child of God: he is both born again, and justified, and sanctified. He that lacks any one of these three things is not a true Christian in the sight of God.' [189] Life after conversion is a new experience for the believer with its new world-view and new spirituality born of God and sanctified by the Holy Spirit. This is always under attack from the Enemy.

The apostle John stresses the grace of holiness, 'He who has been born of God keeps himself' (1 John 5:18). The Christian is one who should have a passion for holiness. The closer we walk with Christ, the less we like to displease Him. To keep ourselves pure is our duty and ought to be our inner desire (1 Timothy 5:22); this includes keeping ourselves from idols (1 John 5:21). This flows from the new nature by regenerating faith that sanctifies the soul, 'elect according to the foreknowledge of God the Father, in sanctification of the Spirit, for obedience and sprinkling of the blood of Jesus Christ (1 Peter 1:2). Holiness is something:

HOLINESS IS PERSONAL

Sanctification starts at conversion, with 'an inheritance incorruptible and undefiled that does not fade away, reserved in heaven for you' (1 Peter 1:4). The vessels of the tabernacle and Temple were to be sanctified unto Jehovah God, i.e. given over to His service completely. They had no other purpose or use. So in Christ we are not our own, we have been bought at

---

189 J.C.Ryle, *Holiness* (Cambridge: James Clarke & Co. Ltd, 1956), p.15.

a price and are separated to Him by grace for service. Sanctification starts with conversion but it continues with consecration (Romans 12:1–2).

HOLINESS IS POWERFUL

Sanctification is separation from all that God hates and from the world and sin (cf. 2 Corinthians 7:1). When we are born again we receive a new nature and a new life principle is implanted. This is the life of God in the soul 'that you may be partakers of the divine nature' (2 Peter 1:4). Holiness is a powerful grace and there is power with it which enables the people of God to cast off the old man and put on the new (Colossians 3:9–10).

HOLINESS IS PRACTICAL

Peter tells us that only obedient saints are holy saints. These two, holiness and obedience, walk together side-by-side: 'As obedient children, not conforming yourselves to the former lusts, as in your ignorance; but as He who called you is holy, you also be holy in all your conduct' (1 Peter 1:14–15). The under-shepherd is *in* the world but not of the world and will endeavour 'to visit orphans and widows in their trouble, and to keep oneself unspotted from the world' (James 1:27). The Greek verb 'to visit' used here is related to the noun for bishop (*episkopos*), implying that pastoral care is practical as well as doctrinal and spiritual. A pastor who supervises God's people does not merely give good sermons but also oversees their care;[190] Spurgeon speaks of the Christian's practical holiness: 'Holiness is like frankincense and myrrh to Christ. Forgive your enemy, and you make Christ glad; distribute of your substance to the poor, and he rejoices; be the means of saving souls, and you give Him to see of the travail of His soul; proclaim His gospel, and you are a sweet savour unto Him.'[191]

---

190 I reject the idea that 'to oversee' is about heavy shepherding and power politics in the local churches.

191 C. H. Spurgeon, *Morning & Evening*, February 15, PM.

HOLINESS IS PROGRESSIVE

There is a process by which we become more Christ-like when obedient to the Word's commands and precepts. Such *practical* sanctification is a process that *should continue* as long as the believer is on earth. He will never achieve perfection or sinlessness on earth, but he should ever be pressing toward that goal. 'For you were once darkness, but now you are light in the Lord. Walk as children of light (for the fruit of the Spirit is in all goodness, righteousness, and truth), finding out what is acceptable to the Lord' (Ephesians 5:8–10). The born-again pastor will show diligence in perfecting holiness that he may be 'preserved blameless at the coming of our Lord Jesus Christ' (1 Thessalonians 5:23; Colossians 3:12–14). The pastor is to grow more like Christ, showing attentiveness to make his calling and election sure. A likeness to the Son of God is sought, and 'by their fruits you shall know them'. Saving faith is to be added and love is to be enlarged (2 Peter 1:5–7). The struggle against indwelling sin is ongoing, so the born-again pastor needs to be under the blood in his daily walk and ministry; 'he who has been born of God keeps himself'. Robert Murray M'Cheyne makes this clear: 'Christ's work is not done [finished] with a soul when He has brought it to pardon—when He has washed it in His own Blood. Oh, no! The better half of salvation remains. His great work of sanctification remains.' [192] Don't be antinomian, rather 'work out your own salvation with fear and trembling' (Philippians 2:12). A life of faith and holiness is encapsulated in the adjectives and phrases Paul uses in Philippians; they are expressive of the characteristics of a holy and happy lifestyle with a Christ-like fruit of the Spirit.

Brethren, whatever things are true, whatever things are noble, whatever things are just, whatever things are pure, whatever things are lovely, whatever things are of good report, if there is any virtue and if there is anything praiseworthy—meditate on these things. (Philippians 4:8)

---

192 R. M. M'Cheyne, *God Makes a Path*, p.91.

Note the (six) adjectives in verse 8:

1. *True:* means honourable or morally attractive. What is *honourable* has no shame on it and needs not to be hidden.

2. *Noble:* truthful, honourable. (Greek *senma*, *'worthy of respect').*

3. *Just* (Greek *dikaia*, means righteous/moral/ good/upright).

4. *Pure* (Greek *hagna*). This word is closely associated with the Greek word for *holy*, i.e. *hagios*, and thus means 'sacred' or 'immaculate'. It would refer to the high moral character of a person's life.

5. *Lovely:* has the idea of that which is admirable or agreeable to behold or consider. Flowers!!

6. *Good report:* has also been translated 'of good repute' or 'fair sounding'.

Also here we have *virtue* (n.) which speaks of moral excellence, i.e. sexual purity, duty, and whatever is praiseworthy and 'something that deserves to be commended'.[193]
These virtues spoken of are worthy of praise, and so pastors are 'to meditate', i.e. 'to deliberate', 'to evaluate', 'to ruminate', on what is true, honest, just, pure, lovely and good. Paul logs all these virtues together: 'If there is any virtue, and if there is anything praiseworthy, meditate on these things'—showing our life of faith is encapsulated in these adjectives and phrases which is expressive the characteristic of a holy and happy lifestyle. He also adds (v.9): 'The things which you learned and received and heard and saw in me, these do, and the God of peace will be with you.' As a saved man Paul exhorts us to follow his lifestyle and holy

---

193 Nelson CD_ROM.

behaviour: not as a recluse or hermit or a monk in a cloistered monastery, or a closeted scholar even, but a co-worker with God (1 Corinthians 3:9) and by 'walking the walk as well as talking the talk'! Rather, pastors are to think and pray, repenting and recommit their lives to Jesus Christ and His truth and call to preach, being earnest and sober and, as (young) Timothy, stirring up the *gift of God* given to him at conversion. The Spirit's presence in us will make the difference between truth and error. The gospel's grace affects, empowers and impacts on us with the spirit 'of power and of love and of a sound mind' (2 Timothy 1:7).

16. Please pray for us

'Life-giving preaching costs the preacher much—death to self, crucifixion to the world, the travail of his own soul. Crucified preaching only can give life. Crucified preaching can come only from a crucified man.' (E. M. Bounds)[194]

'A pastor is one who lays his life on the line. The difference between overseeing elders and the full-time called pastor is the call to leave what may be for some a lucrative calling to serve as a minister of the gospel. A part-time elder faces no such quandary.' (Erroll Hulse)[195]

'Be united in prayer, and give the Lord no rest, till greater things are done by His outstretched arm. "It is no good to preach, if the people do not pray." The prayer which opens heaven and brings down the SPIRIT.' (Asahel Nettleton)

'Woe is me if I do not preach the gospel!' (1 Corinthians 9:16)

'Since we have this ministry, as we have received mercy, we do not lose heart' (2 Corinthians 4:1)

S aul of Tarsus after his conversion and calling (which were nearly simultaneous, Acts 9:1–9, 15–16) was committed to a full-time itinerant preaching, teaching and church planting ministry. His

---

194 Quoted, Stuart Olyott, *The Banner of Truth Magazine*, October, 2021, No. 697, p. 17.
195 Erroll Hulse, 'What is a Pastor?', *Reformation Today*, No. 249, p. 10.

words to the Corinthians confirm his calling and passion for souls: 'For if I preach the gospel, I have nothing to boast of, for necessity is laid upon me; yes, woe is me if I do not preach the gospel!' (1 Corinthians 9:16). These ardent words of Paul's do not sound like a man who makes his legitimate living as a plumber or a medical doctor or scientist, but rather as a man (although a Jew by ethnicity and a tent-maker by trade for income) fully committed to gospel evangelism and church planting. Paul had a new ministry of *Good News* to all (both Jews and Gentiles): 'When I preach the gospel', he said, 'I may present the gospel of Christ without charge, that I may not abuse my authority in the gospel' (1 Corinthians 9:18). Thus, writing again to Corinth later (c. AD 56 or 57), he upholds his calling to ministry: 'Therefore, since we have this ministry, as we have received mercy, we do not lose heart' (2 Corinthians 4:1). With that statement he shows his utter commitment that confirms his out-and-out zeal and consecration: 'But we have renounced the hidden things of shame, not walking in craftiness nor handling the word of God deceitfully, but by manifestation of the truth commending ourselves to every man's conscience in the sight of God' (2 Corinthians 4:2). He speaks as a servant of the New Covenant whose ministry is a ministry of the Spirit and righteousness (cf. 3:6,8,9,17). His calling produced self-denial and a taking-up of his cross: 'For we do not preach ourselves, but Christ Jesus the Lord, and ourselves your bondservants for Jesus' sake' (4:5). He did not embrace this ministry by his own human facility but through the call of the risen Jesus Christ on the Damascus road (Acts 9). At great price he persevered in his calling and was willing to pay the personal costs with its joys and the consequences. The price was high and the way full of obstacles and opposition. There was imprisonment to endure, physical pain as well with foreboding to cope with (2 Corinthians 11:22–29).

Would a twenty-first century pastor cope with all that Paul had to endure? Would he put up with all that hassle? I answer, yes, if he is sure of his calling and trusts in the promises of God all the way. Having put his hand to the plough there would be no turning back.[196] Paul was able the look back on God's grace and assistance and he *did not lose heart*. That is, he did not let weariness or despair hinder his ministry or efforts. To him, suffering was the badge of Christ's servants. He did not avoid reproach, persecution or dishonour for personal gain or preservation. Paul emphasises the solemn responsibility of every servant of Christ to endure hardship and slander in order to make the message of the gospel plain. 'Paul did *not lose heart*. He did not act cowardly, but rather courageously, in the face of seemingly insurmountable barriers.'[197] His words to the churches in Asia (c. AD 47–57) confirm Paul's sense of calling and sacrificial endeavour: 'I became a minister according to the stewardship from God which was given to me for you, to fulfil the word of God … Him we preach, warning every man and teaching every man in all wisdom, that we may present every man perfect in Christ Jesus. To this end I also labour, striving according to His working which works in me mightily' (Colossians 1:25, 28–29).

The pastor's nightmare

The protestant evangelical pastor's nightmare is that a heresy could creep unknowingly into the local church bringing death and not life and overthrowing 'the faith of some'. Hymenaeus and Philetus were preaching 'profane and idle babblings' and had 'strayed concerning the truth, saying that the resurrection is already past; and they overthrow the faith of some' (2 Timothy 2:16–18). This later phrase 'they overthrow the faith of some' highlights how important Bible doctrine is and that it must be embraced by faith, because Jesus declared Himself as the door of salvation for the body as well as the soul. The denial of the truth of Jesus Christ's physical

---

196 He may try, but I believe that the Lord will keep him in his calling both by providence and by persevering grace.
197 Nelson CD_ROM.

resurrection on the third day has done great disservice to the gospel. As a consequence pastors are to preach often on the historical resurrection and its implications (1 Corinthians 15:58).

History as well as theology

The resurrection was not a vision (or hallucination) given to the apostles, but they were persuaded of its reality by witnessing personally to Jesus' glorious miracle. Care needs to be taken when new church attendees request membership and when new leaders (deacons and elders who are to supervise the purity of doctrine in the local assembly) are selected. Peter warned: 'There will be false teachers among you, who will secretly bring in destructive heresies', 'they are presumptuous, self-willed' (2 Peter 2:1, 10). Paul in the Epistles reminds us that there is need of a personal confession of faith from all potential new communicants. It is good to remember in this context Paul's words: 'God ... chose you ... through sanctification ... and *belief* in the truth" (2 Thessalonians 2:13).[198] Biblical orthodoxy is vital! Elders are the under-shepherds of Jesus, the second Person of the Holy Trinity, who watch for our souls; so they need to be theologically literate, full of Bible knowledge and Holy Spirit discernment. As God's messenger the pastor is to be a contender for righteousness and the saving faith given as a gift of grace, while the cults deny the third day resurrection miracle:

- JWs, who say it was spiritual and He is a 'spirit son' of God.

- Christian Scientists say, this was not a literal bodily rising but 'a spiritualising of thought, a new and higher idea of immortality, or spiritual existence'.

---

198 The emphasis is mine.

- Muslims suggest a swoon theory with Jesus reviving in a cold tomb; alternatively, that Jesus did not die on a cross but rather someone else in His place did![199]

- Sceptics have even suggested it was the wrong tomb and therefore a wrong conclusion was propagated.

Patience and wisdom

Much prayer is needed when a new pastor comes to a local church and the old pastor or other pastors are members still. This is an added trial/test for young men out of seminary or new men trying their hand at being under-shepherds and preachers. This is a common problem and one that affects all denominations (and one which spills over into secular organisations). It is a continuing issue in Independency where local churches are not able to fall back on the support of presbyteries. However, denominations with stronger structures of administration still have to legislate regarding this matter. Some Independent churches have written rules to avoid this situation. I understand the Church of England prohibits a retired incumbent to stay in the parish, in order to let the new one have space to serve as necessary. My own experience while in three such pastorates may be of help here. In the first two I replaced the founder pastors (these churches are the trickiest for new men because *founders* are the beloved church planters, can be long serving and the ones to whose rules of administration the consciences of his flock are indelibly fixed). In the third, I followed a good man who remained in membership there. He personally was instrumental in seeing many souls saved over a 31-year period of blessing (not unusual at this period along with other regional churches in the English Midlands,

---

199 See my book, *Engaging with Islam: an evangelical doctrinal perspective* (Day One, 2019).

1945–1980).[200] Church planters, missionaries and retired men from other congregations may also be present, and though not in the eldership they can pose administrative and doctrinal challenges to the younger and inexperienced men. Issues can arise that need extra patience and prayer both by the new man and by the old beloved shepherds. If relationships fail and one or more of the parties leave the congregation, whose fault is it? Probably theirs both! This arrangement (a new shepherd and a retired one) should work out in theory but the practice can be somewhat wanting. A natural tendency in all of us to dislike others (an unsanctified attitude!) because of class, education, nationality, culture, personality, etc., and add to this a new pastor's desire to be 'his own man', etc., can upset the hoped-for equilibrium. In this situation the retired man must grasp that his beloved (old) congregation has (probably) chosen a different personality. This needs to be carefully handled or envisaged beforehand and taken into account if a call is accepted and future blessing gifted. However, much wisdom is necessary when replacing a pastor, because there are 'horses for courses'.

The duty of prayer

When we read the Epistle to the Hebrews we are reminded that prayer helped the writer in times of difficulty to fulfilling his ministry: 'Pray for us; for we are confident that we have a good conscience, in all things desiring to live honourably. But I especially urge you to do this,

---

200 Three examples hold true: (1) in October 1967 the opening service of the *Rugby Evangelical Free Church* took place. Since the church was opened over 370 people have been through the membership of the church. In December 1972, Pastor Peter Jeffery began a 14-year ministry at the church which was exceedingly fruitful; (2) for most of the twentieth century, until 1968, *Pontefract Congregational Church* was in a low state spiritual and numerically. The turning point for the church came in 1968 when the Rev. Bill Dyer was called as pastor. The spiritual development and numerical growth that followed was inspired by gospel preaching; (3) in *Bethel Evangelical Free Church*, Wigston, Leicester in 1940 a missionary, Harold Lewis, held a tent campaign and from that started a regular children's meeting and adult church meeting in a hut on the site of the Youth Hall and bookshop. The present church building was built by the people themselves and the first floor opened in 1955.

that I may be restored to you the sooner' (Hebrews 13:18–19). God's people are asked to exercise a duty of prayer which will be invaluable to pastors and preachers. The apostle Paul requested much prayer so that God's anointing would rest upon him to enable him to fulfil a ministry of preaching the gospel. It is clear from the Scriptures that those who preach the gospel are to be prayed for, and it is the duty of believers to be intercessors on their pastor's and their local church's behalf and to do so regularly and in special seasons of fasting and prayer. This need of helpful prayer vindicates the local church's weekly prayer meetings as well as the believers' own private intercession for the pulpit ministry. That will be powerful before God: 'The effective, fervent prayer of a righteous man avails much' (James 5:16).

When Paul wrote to the New Testament churches he invariably asked the recipients to pray for him; the saints at Corinth were reminded that their prayers helped the apostle through times of difficulty: 'you also helping together in prayer for us' (2 Corinthians 1:11). They were asked to exercise a ministry which would be invaluable to Paul as he served his Master's call and whose value would be truly revealed only in eternity; the church at Rome was asked: 'Strive together with me in prayers to God for me,' in order that he would be free from persecution and his ministry would be a blessing to the Christians in Jerusalem (Romans 15:30–31); the Thessalonian believers were also encouraged to pray for Paul as he concluded his first epistle and said, 'Brethren, pray for us' (1 Thessalonians 5:25). From this we can see that Paul knew the value of intercessory supplication on his behalf. He was conscious of the need of prayer—in fact he longed for such prayer to be made and he asked for such prayers on his behalf. In his Epistle to the Ephesians he requested that he would be enabled to 'open his mouth boldly', thus using the right words when timely opportunities were given to preach the mystery of the gospel (Ephesians 6:19; cf. Colossians 4:3–4). In 2 Thessalonians he hopes that 'the word of the Lord may run swiftly and be glorified' by his ministry

(2 Thessalonians 3:1). It is sometimes forgotten that the call to preach is a vocation—as against a lay or part-time preaching role—and the issue of anointing is paramount. Is this why Paul counselled Timothy: 'No one engaged in warfare entangles himself with the affairs of this life, that he may please him who enlisted him as a soldier' (2 Timothy 2:4)?

Pastors are to meet the contemporary needs of the local church congregations as the Spirit of God leads. They can, and do, lecture at times, but their task is higher and more specialised. They are to preach, teach and exhort re the needs of the hour in local church and state. Thus it is to be borne in mind that Satan attacks them more because of their extraordinary ministry. All Christians have a duty of prayer and share in the success of the gospel—reaping reward (1 Corinthians 9:17a; Matthew 6:4). Prayers of intercession are to be made in Jesus' name for those constantly engaged in Christian ministry (John 16:23–24). Please pray for the men who, like Paul, are saved by grace from unbelief, are called and commissioned, and are willing to forgo worldly rewards and easy living to take the everlasting gospel to the lost and are meant to care for all of Jesus Christ's sheep given him as a good and faithful servant (Luke 16:13; 17:7–10).

'Well done, good and faithful servant'

When our Lord (Matthew 25) speaks of the end times he teaches that eternal rewards will be based on faithfulness to the task appointed, and thus the smallest duty required of the people of God will receive great reward if done to the best of one's ability.

In Colossians 4 we find Paul's final remarks to the church highlight men who had set their hand to the plough with Paul for the kingdom's sake. These biographical notes teach us that God is full of mercy and that his saints are chosen from all walks of life and from all strata of society (1 Corinthians 1:26–31). There we find among Paul's companions a runaway slave called Onesimus (v. 9), engaged in Christian ministry, a restored backslider called John Mark (v. 10), now forgiven and full of zeal, the pastor of the church at Colosse, Epaphras (v. 12), concerned for his flock, a doctor called Luke (v. 14), the author of the Book of Acts; and there are others also who worked with Paul in evangelism. Three men, however, stand out in this closing list and they are John Mark, Demas and Archippus. One is an example of the restoring grace of God while the other two, having put their hand to the plough, are in danger of turning back.

John Mark[201] was the cousin of Barnabas and the writer of the second Gospel. Twelve years prior to this, Mark with Barnabas had left Paul after a disagreement about whether Mark should accompany them on their second missionary journey. In Paul's opinion Mark had been disloyal and cowardly when he had deserted them at the end of their first missionary tour (Acts 15:36–41). Mark's fellowship with Paul was now restored and he was fully engaged in the Lord's work and in full fellowship with the Lord's people. In 2 Timothy 4:11 Paul said that Mark was very useful to him for the ministry, thus assuring us that Mark's restoration to faithfulness was a permanent thing (cf. 1 Peter 5:13). This is encouraging as it tells us never to doubt the grace of God and his promise to keep us from falling (Jude 24). Mark was no longer a liability to Paul and was to be welcomed as a fully committed co-worker of Christ. John Mark was forgiven by God and by Paul. We should not withhold our love from those whom Christ has redeemed and restored. Restoration is a wonderful certainty because God promises it in Christ (Ephesians 3:20–21; Jude 24).

Demas (v. 14b), is something of an enigma. As part of Paul's missionary team he proved to be a valuable helper, but we remember him most because of what Paul wrote of him in 2 Timothy. He is listed there among many of the same companions as are found in Colossians 4, but Timothy is told 'Demas has forsaken me, having loved this present world' (2 Timothy 4:10). This was not only a physical but also a spiritual separation. He had succumbed to worldliness. Sadly, there is no record of

---

201 John was his Hebrew name and Mark his Greek name.

his restoration in the New Testament. This is a reminder that Christians need to make their calling and election sure (2 Peter 1:10).

Archippus (v. 17) was a member of the church in Colosse. Some think he was the son of Philemon and Apphia. Paul spoke to him directly, as he must faithfully fulfil the ministry that he had received in the Lord (v. 17). Notice Archippus was given a:

1. *Public message:* 'Take heed'. Lord Nelson at the Battle of Trafalgar (1805) is said to have told his sailors and marines that 'England expects every man to do his duty,' and this is no less true of the Lord of the churches. The Lord Jesus Christ expects every minister to do his duty by discharging the office given to him whether preaching, teaching, leading, or serving in the local church. All the believers' talents are to be fully utilised in the service of Christ (Matthew 25:14–30). This was the same exhortation that Paul gave to Timothy (1 Timothy 4:16).

2. *Personal message:* 'Take heed to the ministry which you have received in the Lord.' This exhortation was given in support of Archippus and the ministry he was called by God to discharge. What was this ministry? Perhaps he was the elder in charge while Epaphras was with Paul in Rome, or one of the body of elders or deacons? Whatever, he must not run from his responsibility now that Paul had so openly spoken of it! The Lord expects us to do his will when vows have been made.

3. *Pointed message:* 'Fulfil it.' Archippus needed this exhortation, but why? Had he lost heart (cf. 2 Corinthians 4:1,16)? Had he lost his love for the brethren (John 21:15)? Had he found the office that he was called to excessively demanding and now wanted to relinquish it? Had he lost his love for Christ (John 21:16)? We just do not know. But we can be sure that the Holy Spirit meant him to hear this exhortation. God wanted him to complete the work he had received from Christ his Lord.

A better example comes from **Epaphras** (Colossians 4:12). It is generally accepted that Epaphras was the pastor and founder of the church at Colosse. Paul identifies him as 'one of you' (cf. 1:7). He also planted the churches in Laodicea and Hierapolis and was now in Rome visiting Paul in prison to take advice about the situation in the church in Colosse. His heart was warm towards his friends back in Colosse and his prayers were fervent and specific on their behalf. He prayed that they might 'stand perfect and complete in all the will of God' (v. 12). He was a man of prayer. Notice:

(i) *How he prayed:* the phrase 'labouring fervently' speaks of him wrestling and striving in prayer. It is used in Colossians 1:29 of a man toiling at work until he is thoroughly weary and in 1 Corinthians 9:25 of an athlete determined to win the race (we get the English word 'agonising' from it). In 1 Timothy 6:12 it describes the soldier fighting for his life on the battlefield. True intercessory prayer demands self-sacrifice, dedication and determination. Pastors ought to spend time struggling in prayer and supplication; as under-shepherds the flock is given to their care (Acts 20:28).

(ii) *What he prayed:* 'That you may stand perfect and complete in all the will of God'. There is need for the flock to grow up spiritually and to become mature in the things of Christ, remaining firm in the truth. Paul preaches to achieve it (1:28) and Epaphras prays for it to be so. The word 'perfect' (*teleioi*) means 'to finish the process'. There is, in New Testament religion, such a thing as progressive sanctification, i.e. an increase in holiness and the possibility of growing into a deeper love for God, Christ and the brethren (cf. Philippians 3:12–15). The Colossian believers were complete positionally in Christ (2:10), but here the will of God was in view so that they would be able to resist the errors of the 'spoilers' (2:9) and progress in holiness. Epaphras prayed that they would persevere in the faith, in accordance with the will of God, and that their commitment to the truth as it is in Christ Jesus their Lord would continue.

Here are men, highlighted in the pages of Holy Scripture, from whom to learn. Which one of them are we like? Will we hear in the last day, 'Well done, you good and faithful servant' (Matthew 25:21,23)?

Appendix 1:
Ten reasons *not* to be a pastor

'To love to preach is one thing, to love those to whom we preach quite another.' (D. Martyn Lloyd-Jones, *Preaching and Preachers*)

'A man who imagines that because he has a head full of knowledge that he is sufficient for these things had better start learning again. "Who is sufficient for these things?" What are you doing? You are not simply imparting information, you are dealing with souls, you are dealing with pilgrims on the way to eternity, you are dealing with matters not only of life and death in this world, but with eternal destiny.' (D. Martyn Lloyd-Jones, *Preaching and Preachers*)

'In no period of my life have I sought the immediate salvation of men with an aim so direct as I have done these two years. Formerly my immediate aim was the enlightenment of men, hoping that they might be converted some day. Of late my aim has been their conversion there and then. I have gone to the chapels day after day expecting to see men brought to God whilst speaking to them, and God has given me to see wonderful manifestations of His saving power as the result. Some of our warmest, happiest, and most consistent members are men who have been brought to an immediate decision in the course of a single conversation. This directness of aim in regard to the immediate salvation of men has changed my mode of preaching.' (John Griffith, missionary to China, in 1876)

An article which appeared in the *Banner of Truth Trust Magazine* (No. 698, November 2021) called 'Five bad reasons to go into ministry' gives perceptive and helpful advice to all budding preachers.[202] It challenges some false notions which motivate but fail to be good or adequate reasons. I outline them below:

1. You love theology.

2. You love to teach.

3. You are good with people.

4. You are a good communicator.

5. You believe that going into the ministry will somehow be helpful to you.

However, being a pastor is too important a profession to choose wrongly. I have noted that for some, if it is a notion which is not of God but is a self-motivated ambition present in the heart even when the necessary gifts may be apparent, failure is certain.

Another five reasons not to enter the full-time ministry

1. *If not saved*. This is the paramount gift and should be obvious to believers. I have met men who have a story and testimony of a call but they were not born again!

2. *If not called*. Talent and education are necessary, but gifts do not trump grace when it comes to pastoral leadership and spirituality. Test the call (see chapter 2 on the marks of a true call).

---

202 Rebecca Vandoodewaad, *The Banner of Truth magazine*, October 2021.

3. *If your wife is against it.* This is more important than it first appears. Today's wives have their own career ambitions. Married men need to be given to full-time effort with a committed backup from the home and committed wives (Ecclesiastes 4:9–11; Proverbs 31:10–29).[203] In my opinion the contemporary attitude expressed by some pastors' wives 'that I am not *a pastor's* wife but *his* wife!' is a denial of biblical teaching. Many men struggle with the pressures because of this lack of committed and spiritual support in the home.[204]

4. *If a willingness to trust the Lord at all times is missing.* Trusting the Lord is an attitude sourced from faith. It must be put into effect at all times and not only at some times or most times (Psalm 62:8). Relying on God for all necessary grace, spiritual strength, protection, health and material provision demands a constant taking up of the cross of service in this higher calling (Matthew 10:38).

5. *If love for souls is not previously exhibited.* The called pastor will have been a man of evangelism and prayer with compassion for the lost and a willingness to serve others prior to his full conviction of a call.

Paul and preaching

When Paul speaks of preaching God's Word he makes it plain that this is a special calling committed to him. This he states while in prison in Rome:

God ... manifested His word through preaching, which was committed to me according to the commandment of God our Saviour. (Titus 1:3)

---

203 I know of a case where the minister shut down the Lord's Day evening worship service to fit with the need of his busy wife and family.
204 The author is quite aware that this point will not be accepted by some. However, it is his understanding that 'two are better than one' in this special calling.

The phrase 'manifested His word through preaching' explains that from eternity God promised eternal life, through the covenant of grace, which ('in due time') was made clear and obvious in the gospel of Jesus Christ to the world, to both Jews and Gentiles (v. 2; Genesis 3:15; Psalm 32:1–2a; Romans 1:17; Ephesians 3:4–5; 1 Timothy 2:6; 6:15; Galatians 4:4). The phrase 'through preaching, which was committed to me' tells us that the gospel would be revealed and understood through his ministry of preaching and writing. Redemption's mysteries were not fully realised or proclaimed by the prophets of the Old Testament (see Romans 16:25–26; Colossians 1:26a; Isaiah 60:1–3; Habakkuk 2:4; Joel 2:28–29). So Paul and his contemporaries were 'divinely authorised' being called to do this work.

'Preach' is what the pastors *have* to do, viz. *tell it as it is*! This is voiced in common parlance and contains the whole counsel of God in Christ. They are to teach and encourage the faith once given to the saints and this faith resides in the churches which are true to the text and gospel (Jude 3; 1 Timothy 3:15). Without gifts and calling it cannot be done well. It is *'through preaching'* we hear and learn and believe:

How shall they hear without a preacher? And how shall they preach unless they are sent? (Romans 10:14c–15)

To preach is 'to herald', not in weakness but in God's strength. Pastors are to proclaim—not just lecture, but rather to herald—as ambassadors declaring the King's will, commands and mercy by the free offer of salvation, avoiding their own prejudices and politics (2 Timothy 2:4).

Appendix 2:
Stand your ground

The pastor/preacher needs to be aware of apologetics issues. 'Apologetics has to do with defending or making a case for the truth of the Christian faith.'[205] Apologetics and theology are closely linked. Apologetics is simply sincere answers to sincere questions. The Lexicographer confirms that: *apologetics* is derived from the Greek noun *apologia*, that is, a 'verbal defence, or speech in defence'.[206] The Petrine admonition of 1 Peter certainly implies that the Christian faith is capable of reasonable defence (1 Peter 3:15b): 'Always be ready to give a defence to everyone who asks you for a reason for the hope that is in you, with meekness and fear.' In the book *Five Views on Apologetics*, S. B. Cowan writes: 'Apologetics is concerned with the defence of the Christian faith against charges of falsehood, inconsistency, or credulity.'[207] He continues: 'As concerning the Christian faith, [then] apologetics has to do with defending, or making a case for the truth of the Christian faith.'[208]

---

205 S. B. Cowan, ed. *Five Views on Apologetics* (Grand Rapids, MI: Zondervan Publishing House, 2000), p. 8.

206 J. H. Thayer, *Greek–English Lexicon of the New Testament* (Grand Rapids, MI: Associated Publishers and Authors, no date given); cf. Acts 25:16; 2 Corinthians 7:11; Philippians 1:7, 17; and 2 Timothy 4:16; with a dative of the person who is to hear the defence. Cf. 1 Corinthians 9:3; 1 Peter 3:15; Acts 22:1.

207 S. B. Cowan, ed. *Five Views on Apologetics*, p. 8f.

208 The apostle Paul defended himself before the Roman officials in Acts 24:10 and 25:8. The Greek verb (*apologeomai*) occurs ten times in the New Testament, and the Greek noun (*apologia*) occurs eight times. This shows that the Christian preacher is 'under obligation to propound and defend their faith before a hostile world'.

A biblical approach to apologetics believes 'the Christian revelation in Scripture is the framework through which all experience is interpreted and all truth is known' (Cornelius Van Til).[209] To say 'God exists' is placing oneself where the Bible is. So what do reformed evangelicals believe? Faith is divine revelation and 'God's truth is the only object of faith' (Van Til).[210] So Christians proclaim propositional truth believing that the sinner is incapable of an unprejudiced, unbiased and impartial act of the mind. Reason and logic have their place but they need to be subservient to Scripture. Christians must not be ashamed to appeal to Scripture.

Presuppositional apologetics

When debating about God and creation Christians are to take a stand using arguments that God exists and speaks to humanity through the Bible as well as through the created world around us. Daily all of us make decisions on the suppositions we hold, e.g. we expect the sun to rise in the morning and thus we get ready to act on that opinion. Our lives are ruled by our suppositions. Some suppositions are spurious, some instinctive. Propositional ideas are those which rule our opinions, attitudes, ideas, and are the basis of our personal world-view.

In the *Origins* debate Christians should do not go out of their way to try to prove that God exists but simply accept it because man is made in the image of God (Genesis 1:26). Creationists accept that all of Adam's descendants possess an innate sense of God (i.e. an inborn sense) which cannot be seriously denied (Romans 1:19–20). Christians appeal to this inborn sense of God because the conscience is a witness to God's existence. To refuse this as valid proof is to deny believing Christians the right to stand in their debate with atheism with the Bible in their hands. The

---

209 J. R. Beeke, 'Cornelius Van Til and Apologetics', *The Banner of Truth Magazine*, 1992, No. 342, p. 20.
210 See Cornelius Van Til, *The Reformed Pastor and Modern Thought* (Phillipsburg, NJ: Presbyterian and Reformed Publishing Co., 1971), p. 30.

atheist comes to the debate with *his* presupposition, viz. that there is no God. To deny the creationist *his* theistic position is to give the atheist an unjust advantage and to dispossess the Christian of his God-given 'sword of the Spirit and shield of faith'.

The concept of revelation

Evidential apologetics is also useful in the creation debate and so the present-day practice of pairing a Bible believing scientist with an evangelical theologian apologist is to be welcomed. This duo enhances the depth of argument against unbelief; however, the scientist's contribution can only assist the witness of the Word of God. This is because it relies on data that may change or be superseded by the discovery of new laws of physics, biology, etc. Even the best science cannot, and does not, have the authority of the inerrant Word of God, because the concept of special revelation is central to Christianity. Thus the people of God have a source from which to draw in order to have something to say about our origins as humans and the life of God in the soul of men. It is sad to reflect that what is most important in the *origins debate* for some Christians is not what the Bible says but what the scientists say! Another aspect to be grasped here is that scientific evidence is not the God-ordained path to eternal life, for 'faith comes by hearing, and hearing by the word of God' (Romans 10:17). Al Mohler states this well:

'In the final analysis, the ultimate authority for preaching is the authority of the Bible as the Word of God. Without this authority, the preacher stands naked and silent before the congregation and the watching world. If the Bible is not the Word of God, the preacher is involved in an act of self-delusion or professional pretension. Standing on the authority of Scripture, the preacher declares a truth received, not a message invented. The teaching office is not an advisory role based in religious expertise but a prophetic function whereby God speaks to His people.'[211]

211 Al Mohler, *He is Not Silent* (Chicago: Moody, 2008), p. 72.

As the children of God we are to observe God's revealed essence in the created order. However, this alone will not bring salvation as no one can know God except through the Scripture (the Bible) revelation and also with the aid of the Spirit of God working through faith and assisting reason. Rather we must be as Martin Luther who trusted the 'external Word' (the Scriptures) before the ideas, pronouncements and authority of Councils, Synods and all who rule whether for universities or church.

Appendix 3:
A gospel church

'The True Nature of a Gospel Church and its Government', by Owen was written in 1689.[212] It has 11 chapters and covers the topics that embrace the whole of church polity, function and order. I supply a summary below:

In his *The Visible Church Defined*, Owen tells us that the Roman Empire under one monarch gave rise to 'a pretended visible ruling catholic church'. Thus 'the visible church [was] moulded and fashioned into an image of the old Roman pagan empire, as it was foretold it should be, Revelation 13:12–15'.[213] He *defines the church* as

(i) A place of *separation*: Owen says regeneration is required for 'an entrance into the church or kingdom'. This distinguishes the church from all other kingdoms.

(ii) A place of *sanctification*: those guilty of habitual sin and scandalous sins cannot be part of the visible church. Six qualifications for local church membership are given. The church is a voluntary society.

(iii) A place of *supervision*: the rule of the church is the exercise of power given to it from Christ, but this power is 'over the souls and consciences of men only'.[214] The power of the keys for binding and loosing is expressly granted to the whole church (Matthew 18:17–18).

---

212 John Owen, *'The True Nature of a Gospel Church and its Government'*, in *Works of John Owen*, ed. W. H. Goold (London: The Banner of Truth Trust, 1968), Vol. 16, pp. 3–208.
213 Ibid, p. 201.
214 Ibid, p. 31.

(iv) A place of *salvation*: the church exists to preach the Word for evangelism to the world, and to preach the Word for edification—to the professors; thus it is to baptise professors and their infants; to eat the Supper; to preserve the truth and gospel.

Its officers identified

(i) Pastors: In the New Testament bishops, presbyters or elders are the same persons and officers with the same function. 'He who is the pastor is the bishop, the elder, the teacher of the church.'[215] There is a plurality of elders.[216] Owen requires five qualities and assigns in excess of ten duties to pastors.[217] The act of calling a pastor is the duty of the church. They are to be chosen by the people. Owen examines the meaning of *cheirotoneo* (Acts 14:23) which he says means 'to stretch forth the hand'.[218] The right to rule and teach is given from the church to the officers. The pastoral ministry is absolutely necessary to the church for its preservation 'hence the first duty of a church without officers is to attain them, according to rule'.

(ii) Teachers: He discusses four ideas regarding teachers but favours the one that says that a teacher is a distinct officer in the church; his office is of the same kind with that of the pastor. However, there may be teachers in a church called only to the work of teaching.

(iii) Ruling elders possess 'the keys of order' that is the *spiritual right* to preach, administer at the sacrament and to bind and loose the consciences of men. The duty of elders is to rule, watch, warn, visit the sick and

---

215 Ibid, p. 48.
216 Owen agrees, p. 46, that for administrative purposes a 'president' may be chosen among elders/bishops but all are equals and there are no archbishops or archdeacons, etc. in the New Testament.
217 Ibid, p. 51 and pp. 74–88.
218 Ibid, p. 60f.

imprisoned, advise and care; it is their duty to acquaint the teaching elder/ pastor with the state of the flock, to meet with the teaching and other elders, to preserve unity.

(iv) Deacons: 'This office of deacon is an office of service, which gives not any authority or power in the rule of the church.'[219]

Its power clarified

The rule of the church is the exercise of power given to it from Christ. The communication of church power is given to all members as privileged sons of God even when they meet as twos or threes. The power of the keys for binding and loosing is expressly granted to the whole church (Matthew 18:17–18). The power of the church towards its members is *admission*, *rule* and *exclusion*. Excommunication is an institution of Christ and there is nothing more wholesome or useful to the souls of men. The church being a voluntary society has a lawful right to deal with its own legitimate interests, but this does not take away any right that its members have. The act of excommunication is designed to reach the minds and consciences. There is only one kind of excommunication, i.e. a separation from all participation in church order, worship and privileges is the only excommunication spoken of in the Scriptures.[220] The elders and not the deacons exert the act of power. Yet in 1 Corinthians 5 the whole church is involved, so excommunication without the consent of the church is 'a mere nullity'.[221]

The communion of churches recognised

Churches of like faith and order 'ought to hold communion among themselves' to promote the 'edification of the catholic church'. This

---

219 Ibid, p. 147.
220 Ibid, p. 165.
221 i.e. 'a mere nothing', ibid, p. 166.

communion is incumbent on every church. This communion is with all churches everywhere but can only be known practically by 'local' churches. 'This is the true and only *catholicism* of the church.'[222] This communion will manifest itself in the churches gathering in synod for advice and for assistance. The power and authority of synods is threefold. They have (1) a *declarative* power, (2) a *constitutive* power of appointing or ordaining things to be believed, (3) an *executive* power.

---

222 Ibid, pp. 185–186.

Appendix 4:
The Lord's Day-Sabbath

'The incomparable significance of the Sabbath day is shown in that this is the very first time the word holy is used in the Bible. The seventh day was lifted up above the plane of the other days.' (Douglas Kelly)[223]

'He takes away the seventh day but does He leave no day for the saints to gather for worship? The seventh day is gone with its shadows but the divine stamp is there upon the first day if we would acknowledge it.' (John Bunyan)[224]

'I was in the Spirit on the Lord's day.' (Revelation 1:10)

The children of Israel worshipped on the seventh day just as their descendants the Jews today, while Christians worship on the first day of the week. Why this difference? Why the change of day for Christian worship from the last to the first day of the week? The Seventh Day Adventists insist on a Saturday Sabbath, so why do New Testament believers not agree with their keeping Saturday as the Lord's Day-Sabbath? Is this because of history? Is it because the Emperor Constantine Christianised the Roman Empire in the fourth century AD and made the day of the sun (Sunday) a religious holiday, as they suggest? Or

---

223 D. F. Kelly, *Creation and Change* (Fearn, Ross-shire: Christian Focus, 1997), p.237.
224 John Bunyan (1628–1688), 'Questions about the Nature and Perpetuity of the Seventh-Day Sabbath', *The Works of John Bunyan* (London: Blackie and Son, 1861), Vol.2, p.382.

is it because of theology? Is evangelical worship grounded on theological imperative and biblical clarity? Let us consider.

Divine distinction: Exodus 20:11

We find the Ten Commandments, or, as the Jews describe them, the 'ten words', in Exodus 20.[225] They were written by the hand of God and given to Moses the man of God and leader of the children of Israel on Mount Sinai in tablets of stone. The first tablet, it is normally assumed, contained commandments one to four and the second tablet housed the remaining six. The fourth and largest commandment on the Sabbath day is in the first tablet. The Puritan George Swinnock (1627–1673) wrote: 'The first commandment teacheth us the object of worship; the second, the matter of worship; the third, the manner of worship; the fourth, the time of worship.'[226] The time of worship is no less important than the matter or the manner of our worship, because we read: *'Remember the Sabbath day, to keep it holy.'* God has given a day for a Sabbath (rest). Christians need to grasp afresh that there is a *time* to be holy. The whole day is to be set aside for God and His worship. The Lord's half-day is an insult to Him. Is our God too small? Do we think that one hour or so is sufficient to honour the Maker of heaven and earth, the God of our salvation? Are we not grateful for our salvation? Do we not hunger and thirst after Him and His righteousness (Psalm 42:1)? God blessed the seventh day and by doing so He blessed the *specific time-period*. One contemporary Jewish writer notes: 'While the pagan world was familiar with the idea of holiness in particular places in space, Judaism emphasised the concept of holiness in time.'[227] One day in seven is 'a

---

225 Three categories of Law can be discerned in the Old Testament, viz. moral, ceremonial, civil. J. F. Bayes, *The Threefold Division of the Law* (Newcastle upon Tyne: The Christian Institute, 2005). The Baptist 1689 Confession and the Westminster and Savoy Confessions of Faith concur.

226 George Swinnock, *Works* (Edinburgh: The Banner of Truth Trust, 1992), p. 222.

227 Shubert Spero, *The Jewish Bible Quarterly*, 'Shabbat: Three Stages in Israel's Experience', Vol. 32:3, July–September 2004, p. 169, n. 5.

portion of time set apart, by divine appointment, for the observance and performance of the solemn worship of God', it is the ultimate end of our creation. John Owen says: 'By the law of nature we are bound to worship God.'[228]

Genesis 2:3

Exodus 20:11 points back to creation itself: 'In six days the LORD made the heavens and the earth.' Moses takes his readers back to the beginning, back to the creation account, and leaves them in no doubt that the command to keep one day in seven holy is a creation ordinance, i.e. a principle established and a precept given by God for all humanity. At the beginning, God separated one day from the other six. He made it different when He blessed it and sanctified it: 'Then God blessed the seventh day and sanctified it' (Genesis 2:3). This verb 'sanctified' means 'to be holy' (Hebrew *qds*). It is the first time it is used in the Bible, and it bears the basic meaning 'to set apart', 'to be distinct'; thus, 'to consecrate'. He made that day different by setting it apart from all the rest. The seventh day, in other words, is to be different from the other six days. This meant that it was exalted above other days and it was preferred before them. Thus, we read 'Remember the Sabbath *day* to keep it holy' (Exodus 20:8) because God blessed the seventh day and He consecrated it and He blessed the *specific time-period*. The seventh day marks Adam's first full day in the garden. In Adam 'humanity spends the first day of existence in God's Sabbath, worshipping and enjoying Him'.[229] When God *sanctified* this day He gave it as a day set apart for worship and sacred rest.

---

228 John Owen, *Works*, Vol. 18, p. 332. 'The description of the seventh day in the schema is solely in terms of God. The climax of creation is not man on the sixth day but God's rest on the seventh', G. Dickson in D. Kell, *The Lord's Day in Secular Society* (Edinburgh: Rutherford House, 1999), p. 28.
229 J. D. Currid, *Genesis*, Vol. 1 (Darlington: Evangelical Press, 2003), p. 94.

Deuteronomy 5:15

We find the Ten Commandments written again in Deuteronomy 5:12–15 where they are the same as in Exodus 20 except that the fourth commandment has been enlarged:

Remember that you were a slave in the land of Egypt, and LORD your God brought you out from there by a mighty hand and by an outstretched arm; therefore the LORD your God commanded you to keep the Sabbath day. (Deuteronomy 5:15)

Why this addition? God wants them to know that the Sabbath is a memorial of emancipation and is grounded in redemption. Deuteronomy 5 points to the greater and future deliverance to come through Jesus Christ the Messiah—the Prophet like unto Moses (Deuteronomy 18:15)—and His glorious resurrection from the dead. The holiness of the Christian Lord's Day-Sabbath is connected to creation and *also* to redemption. This model is picked up in the New Testament and thus the change of day from the seventh to the first day of the week is grounded there and anticipates the resurrection of Jesus Christ on the first day of the week. The resurrection gives religious significance to Sunday and makes it holy. God has rescued His people, through His Son, from the bondage of sin and death. The resurrection day is indispensably important to Christian worship. The Christian Lord's Day-Sabbath memorialises the resurrection, just as the Lord's Supper is a memorial of Christ's death (1 Corinthians 11:23). So deliverance for the children of Israel from Egypt gave sanction to the Sabbath institution under the Old Testament and the resurrection of Jesus Christ (Revelation 1:10) established a new Sabbath day for the church in the New Testament era (economy/dispensation). This was the belief and practice of the second-century church. Justin Martyr, writing around AD 160, comments:

But we all hold this common gathering on Sunday, since it is the first day, on which God transforming darkness and matter made the Universe, and Jesus Christ our

Saviour on the same day rose from the dead. For they crucified Him on the day before Saturday, and on the day after Saturday, He appeared to His apostles and disciples.[230]

John Owen notes that Justin Martyr used the word Sunday and not Sabbath, for 'had he said "on the Sabbath", the Gentiles would have concluded it to have been the Judicial (Jewish) Sabbath. To have called it to them "the Lord's Day"... they would not have known what he meant.'[231] See then how the Bible is united in this matter of a Christian Sabbath; it memorialises the rest of God at creation and the deliverance wrought by the work of Christ in redemption.

The Lord's Day and apostolic authority and practice

The apostles found direction regarding the Sabbath principle when the Lord arose from the dead. There were some believers who no doubt kept both Saturday and Sunday as Sabbaths in the early days of the New Testament era, but the apostles established, with Christ's authority, first-day worship. Let us now look to the New Testament for proof of this.

The risen Saviour appeared on *the first day of the week* after His resurrection, to Mary Magdalene (John 20:1). We note also that the apostles came together on the first resurrection evening (John 20:19). Note how the Holy Spirit gives double emphasis to the exact day and time in verse 19, lest we miss the point being made. A week later (John 20:26) Thomas is with the twelve, having missed the first meeting with the risen Christ, and the same thing happens: 'Jesus came, the doors being shut, and stood in the midst, and said, "Peace to you!"' He sanctified their coming together with His presence and blessing. John Bunyan

---

230 Justin Martyr, *Ancient Christian Writers*, 'The First and Second Apologies' (New York: Paulist Press, 1997), p.71. Bauckham is sure 'that in the *Didache*, Ignatius, and the Gospel of Peter [Lord] is a technical term in fairly widespread use at least in Syria and Asia Minor, designating the first day of the week as the Christian day of regular corporate worship', the Lord's Day, p.231.

231 John Owen, *Works*, Vol.18, p.283.

(the Baptist preacher) is convinced that the phrase 'after eight days' (John 20:26) confirms this day is the chosen new Sabbath established by the Holy Spirit.[232] This was the start of a sanctified pattern of worship and it became the custom of the first church in Jerusalem after the ascension.

Turning to *Acts 2:1* and the day of Pentecost, we find them all together again and this was also on the first day of the week, for Pentecost was always on the next day after the seventh day Sabbath.[233] So the time of new covenant worship is revealed. The Puritan John Owen remarks this day was owned by Christ and given His title or why was it called the new day of worship?[234] In *Acts 20:7* the apostles and the saints, whilst at Troas, came together to break bread on the first day of the week (Sunday). The context here is that of apostolic worship with the breaking of bread (the Lord's Supper) and preaching. This is not the Roman Catholic mass but the simple, yet profound, remembering of the Lord's death *till He comes* (1 Corinthians 11:26). This was the continuation of a new practice established by the apostles after Pentecost (Acts 2:44–47) and adapted to worship in the provinces of Asia (Acts 17:2). The apostle Paul, writing to the Corinthians (*1 Corinthians 16:1–2*), makes it clear that the gathering of the people of God on *the first day of the week* was now the preferred time of worship. It was commanded by the Saviour through Paul (1 Corinthians 14:37; 1 Thessalonians 4:8) and grants the universal adoption of this new practice for the New Testament churches. Apostolic authority for this change of day is found also in 1 Corinthians 11:23, and the words '*For I received from the Lord that which I also delivered to you.*' The apostles had the infallible guidance of the Spirit: 'What they ordained was no less of divine institution if it had been appointed

---

232 John Bunyan (1628–1688), 'Questions about the Nature and Perpetuity of the Seventh-Day Sabbath', *The Works of John Bunyan* (London: Blackie and Son, 1861), Vol. 2, p. 374 John Bunyan, *Questions*, Vol. 2, p. 374.
233 Ibid, p. 374.
234 Owen, *Works 23* Vol. 18, p. 424.

by Christ in His own person.'[235] From all the above the apostle John's words in Revelation 1:10 are to be clearly understood as referring 'to the day of the Lord's resurrection, the first day of the week, set aside by the apostles under the direction of the Holy Spirit as a day of special worship and consecration to take the place of the seventh day Sabbath of the old dispensation'.[236]

The post-apostolic church

This pattern established by the apostles was the model used by the post-apostolic churches in the second, third and fourth centuries AD. Ignatius' 'Letter to the Magnesians', section 9, written in the second century AD makes this clear: 'If, therefore, those who were brought up in the ancient order of things have come to the possession of a new hope, no longer observing the Sabbath, but living in the observance of the Lord's Day, on which also our life has sprung up again by Him and by His death.' *The Didache* states: 'But every Lord's Day do ye gather yourselves together, and break bread, and give thanksgiving after having confessed your transgressions, that your sacrifice may be pure.'[237]

English Puritans

John Bunyan believed that the change in day had become customary in the churches by Paul's time. When Bunyan wrote about the Lord's Day in 1685 he dealt with the change of day from the seventh to the first, calling his work *Questions about the Nature and Perpetuity of the Seventh-Day Sabbath*.[238] He said Sunday has the badge of the Lord's glory upon it because divine grace is put into it, as it is the day of weekly commemoration of the resurrection (Matthew 28:1–10).[239] The first day

---

235 Owen, *Works*, Vol. 18, p. 425.
236 Hoeksema, *Behold He Cometh*, p. 34.
237 *The Didache*, Chapter 14; https://www.newadvent.org/fathers/0714.htm
238 John Bunyan, *Questions*, Vol. 2.
239 Ibid, p. 373.

of the week became the worship day for the New Testament churches because of the resurrection. Quoting Hebrews 4:10, Bunyan says that Christ's day of rest is the Sunday for on it He has ceased from His own works having conquered death by His rising again. Sunday being the day of rest for the Son of God, 'it must be the day of rest for His church also'.[240] Richard Baxter wrote extensively on the change of day and its dominical authority, saying that the apostles did actually separate and appoint the first day of the week for holy worship. The Christians of the apostolic age knew before the Scriptures were written that the Lord's Day was set apart as holy. There was no need to tell them what they were already practising. The New Testament and the universal tenor and practice of the churches are what must be followed.[241]

Conclusion

Bunyan sums all this up saying that Sunday is the first day of church worship, because *(i)* Christ began it on *that* day (John 20:19), *(ii)* the Holy Ghost seconded it on *that* day (Acts 2:1ff), *(iii)* the churches practised it on *that* day (Acts 20:11), and *(iv)* Revelation 1:10 sanctions *that* day to the churches to the end of the world.[242] There is an obvious accumulative message in the New Testament that the first day of the week has become the market day of the soul. Why do Christians worship on Sunday? I hope what has been said has been clear and the reasons for the change of day are obvious to you, so much so that you are left in no doubt that what Christendom does when it sanctifies the first day of the week for the worship of God is by the Lord Jesus Christ's command to the churches, this being clearly seen from the New Testament and from church history.

---

240 Ibid, p.371.
241 Richard Baxter, *Practical Works* (London: James Duncan, 1830), Vol. 13, pp.370–414.
242 John Bunyan, *Questions*, Vol. 2, p.378.

Appendix 5:
Bible wisdom
(counselling help)

Promises in the Bible

Remember the word to Your servant, upon which You have caused me to hope.
(Psalm 119:49)

'Whatever your special need, find some promise in the Bible suited to it. Are you faint and feeble because your way is rough and you are weary? Here is the promise—"He gives power to the faint.' When you read a promise, take it back to the great Promiser, and ask him to fulfil his own word. Are you seeking after Christ, and thirsting for closer communion with him? This promise shines like a star upon you—"Blessed are those who hunger and thirst for righteousness, for they shall be filled" (Matthew 5:6). Take that promise to the throne continually; do not plead anything else, but go to God over and over again with this—"Lord, thou hast said it, do as thou hast said." Are you distressed because of sin, and burdened with the heavy load of your iniquities? Listen to these words: "I have blotted out, like a thick cloud, your transgressions, and like a cloud, your sins" (Isaiah 44:22). Are you afraid lest you should not be able to hold on to the end, lest, after having thought yourself a child of God, you should prove a castaway? If that is your state, take this word of grace to the throne and plead it: "'The mountains shall depart and the hills be removed, but My kindness shall not depart from you, nor shall My covenant of peace be removed,' says the LORD, who has mercy on you" (Isaiah 54:10). If you have lost the sweet sense of the Saviour's presence, and are seeking him with a sorrowful heart, remember the promises: "For a mere moment have I forsaken you, but with great mercies will I gather you" (Isaiah 54:7). Feast your faith upon God's own word, and whatever your fears or wants, repair to the Bank of Faith saying, "Remember the word to Your servant, upon which You have caused me to hope" (Psalm 119:49).'[243]

Topic	OLD Testament	NEW Testament
Anger	Genesis 4:6	1 John 3:12 Ephesians 4:26
Anxious	Exodus 14:14 Jeremiah 17:8	Luke 12:29 Philippians 4:6–7
Bereaved	Genesis 3: 3, 17–19; 5:5 Genesis 25:8–10 Ruth 1:5 Job 1:21 Psalm 23:4 Ecclesiastes 7:2–4; 12:7	John 11:25–26 John 14:1–3 Romans 3:23 1 Corinthians 15:50–57 Philippians 3:21 1 Thessalonians 4:13–18 Revelation 21:4
Bitter	Habakkuk 3:17–18 Lamentations 3:19 Proverbs 14:10	Ephesians 4:31 Hebrews 12:15
Broken-hearted	Psalm 34:18; 51:17; 147:3 Proverbs 15:13 Isaiah 61:1	Matthew 5:4 Romans 8:28–30, and 31–32 1 Peter 5:7–9

---

243 Spurgeon, *Morning & Evening*, April 28, am.

Contentment	Psalm 17:15 Psalm 116:1 Proverbs 19:23 Isaiah 53:11	1 Timothy 6:6
Danger	Psalm 46:1–3 Psalm 62:8 Proverbs 4:23–27	Matthew 5:21–21 Romans 8:35 Ephesians 6:10
Death of a child	2 Samuel 12:19–22 Psalm 107:30–31 Isaiah 54:1, 5–8 Isaiah 66:17–25	Matthew 19:14 Luke 8:52 John 11. 11–13 Acts 2:39 Revelation 21:1–5
Death of a spouse	Genesis 23:2 and 35:16–20 Job 19:25–26	1 Thessalonians 4:16 Philippians 1:23b 1 Corinthians 15: Revelation 22:1–5
Disappointment	Genesis 42:36 Psalm 138:8 Proverbs 3:5–7 Job 1:20–21	Romans 8:31 and 37–39 2 Corinthians 1:3 Philippians 1:6 and 12 Hebrews 6:9–12 1 John 4:16
Distressed	Job 21:34 Psalm 119:50, 82; 147:3 Habakkuk 2:4; 3:17–18	Matthew 11:28 Luke 22:31 2 Corinthians 4:8, 9 16–18 Romans 8:28–29, 34; 15:4–5 Hebrews 4:14–16; 7:25
Facing death	Psalm 23:4 Psalm 30:10 Proverbs 3:5–7	John 11:25–26 John 14:18 Romans 8:38–39 Philippians 1:23b 1 Corinthians 15:55 Hebrews 13:6 Revelation 20:6

Fear	Genesis 32:11 Exodus 20:20 Joshua 10:18 Ruth 3:11 Psalm 17:15 Job 1:9 Psalm 19:9 and 34:9 Proverbs 9:10	Hebrews 13:6 1 Peter 2:17 1 John 4:18
Guidance	Psalm 3:4 Psalm 32:8–9 Psalm 119:27,34 and 105 Proverbs 3:5–7 Proverbs 16:3	Mark 14:38 Luke 11:9 John 15:16 Philippians 4: 9 and 2 Timothy 1:13 Jude 3
Holy Spirit	Job 33:4 Psalm 51:11 Isaiah 40:13 Isaiah 61:1 Joel 2:28–32 Zechariah 4:6	Mark 1:8 Luke 11:13 John 4:24; 14:16–17; 15:26; 16:8, 13–15. Acts 1:5, 8; 2:4; 10:24 Romans 8:14, 16,16 Galatians 5:22–25 Ephesians 1:13: 4:30 Hebrews 10:15 1 John 4:2; 5:7 Revelation 1:10
Humiliation	Psalm 25:9; 34:2; 51:1–4; 69:32 Proverbs 3:34; 11:2; 16:19; 28:3; 29:23	James 4:6, 10 1 Peter 5:6 1 John 1:9

Hope	Psalm 31:15; 38:15; 42:11; 43:5; 57:3; 71:5; 147:11 Proverbs 26:12 Jeremiah 31:17 Lamentations 3:21–24, 26, 31–33	John 11:25–26 Romans 5:5–4: 8:24–25; 15:13 1 Corinthians 13:13; 15:19 Galatians 5:5 1 Thessalonians 13 2 Timothy 4:6–8 Titus 2:13 Hebrews 6:19;10:32 1 John 3:3
Illness		James 5:13–18
Loneliness		Matthew 28:20
Peace	Exodus 14:14 Numbers 6:26; 25:12 Judges 6:23 Psalm 4:8; 85:8–10; 122:6 Isaiah 26:3; 48:2	Luke 10:5 John 14:27; 20:21, 26 Philippians 4:6–7 Colossians 3:15 2 Thessalonians 3:16 Hebrews 13:20
Persecution	Genesis 4:8; 27:41; 31:1–2; 37:11, 28; 39:1, 20–21 Exodus 1:22 2 Kings 24:1 Psalm 7:1; 31:15; 119:86 Jeremiah 17:18	Matthew 5:10–11, 44; 10:21–22. Mark 13:13 Luke 21:19 Romans 12:14 Galatians 4:28 2 Timothy 1:8; 4:6–8, 17–18 1 Peter 3:13–17; 5:7–9 Revelation 2:8–11; 3:7–13; 12:11; 14:12

Perseverance	Deuteronomy 31:16; 33:27 Joshua 1:9 Job 2:3; 29:14a Psalm 23:3, 6; 34:19; 37:3–4; 137: Isaiah 30:21:41:10; 43:2 Daniel	John 14:16 Romans 5:3; 8:25; 12:12 1 Corinthians 3:11–15; 10:12–13 2 Corinthians 4:1, 16 Colossians 1:11 James 5:7–11 1 Peter 4:7 2 Peter 1:6 Hebrews 10:36–39; 11:6; 30–40; 12:1–11 Jude 3, 20–21
Prayer	Numbers 6:24–26 1 Samuel 1:27 1 Kings 9:3 Job 22:27 Psalm 4:1; 39:12; 55:1; 88:13 Proverbs 15:8: 28:9Jonah 2:7	Matthew 6:9–15 Mark 9:29; 11:17 Luke 11:5–7; 18:13 John 14:13–14; 15:15; 16:24; 171, 9, 20 Ephesians 3:14–21 Colossians 4:2–3 2 Thessalonians 5:23 Philippians 4:4–7 Ephesians 6:18 Colossians 4:2–4 James 1:5–8; 5:13–18 1 Peter 5:10–11 1 John 5:14–15 Jude 24–25

Providence	Genesis 16:7; 22:8; 37:28; 50:20 Exodus 2:9–10 Ruth 1:5 Psalm 32:8; 91:3 Proverbs 3:5	Luke 22:31–32 Romans 8:28–31;15:13 1 Corinthians 1:8–9 2 Corinthians 16:13–14 Philippians 1:12 1 Thessalonians 5:24 2 Timothy 2:13 Hebrews 13:16 Revelation 2:
Renewal	Psalm 71:20 Psalm 80:14, 18 Psalm 119:37, 88, 107, 159 Isaiah 43:3; 55:1–3 Jeremiah 33:3 Habakkuk 3:2 Zechariah 12:10	John 21:16–17 1 John 5:4 Revelation 2:5, 7
Sanctification	Joshua 3:5 Job 42:5–6 Psalm 138:8 Joel 2:16 Malachi 3:17	John 17:17 2 Corinthians 7:1 Ephesians 5:26 1 Thessalonians 5:23 Hebrews 13:12 James 1:2–4 1 Peter 3:15
Sleeplessness	Esther 6:1 Job 33:15 Psalm 4:8; 44:23 Proverbs 6:4; 20:13 Song of Songs 5:2	1 Thessalonians 5:6 1 Peter 5:7

Spiritual warfare	Genesis 39:21 I Kings 13:18–22 Job I and 2; 5:8; 13:15 Psalm 121 Daniel	Matthew 4:1–11 Luke 22: 31–32 2 Corinthians 2:11; 11:3 Ephesians 2:2; 6:1–18 I Timothy 4:1 James 4:7 I Peter 5:8 Revelation 12:1–6
Suffering	Genesis 3:16 I Chronicles 4:9–10 Job 14:1 Psalm 25:18; 138:7–8	Matthew 24:13 Romans 8:18 2 Corinthians 1:5–11 Philippians 3:10 James 5:13–18 I Peter 4:1–2, 12–19 Revelation 22:12
Trials	Exodus 14:14	Matthew 11:28–30 Ephesians 6:10–18 James 1:2–4, 12–14 I Peter 4:12–19 Revelation
Weak in faith		I Corinthians 16:13 Ephesians 6:10 2 Timothy 2:1
Weary		2 Corinthians 1:20; 4:1, 7–10, 16 Galatians 6:9 2 Thessalonians 3:13 Hebrews 12:3 Revelation 2:2–4
Wisdom	Proverbs 1:7; 3:21 Ecclesiastes 2:6; 7:12	I Corinthians 1:30; 2:1–10 Colossians 4:5 James 1:5; 3:7

Witnessing	Exodus 20:16 Psalm 19:1–6 Proverbs 14:5 Isaiah 55:4	Matthew 24:14 John 8:18; 15:27 Acts 10:43 Romans 8:18 Philippians 1:8
Worried	Isaiah 30:21;41:10; 43:2	1 Corinthians 7:22 1 Peter 5:7
Worship	Exodus 20:1–11 Psalm 5:7; 25:1; 29:2	John 4:24 Revelation 14:7

Appendix 6: Bibliography

Understanding of the call to full-time ministry topic is of utmost importance for pastors to grasp. Assured calling and good government will aid good ministry and encourage harmony under good order and competent leadership. As Hulse has said, 'There is no class of men and no profession under heaven more important than that of Pastors' (Erroll Hulse, 'What is a pastor?' Reformation Today magazine, No. 249, 2012, p. 9).

Adams, J. E., *Pulpit Speech* (USA: Presbyterian and Reformed Publishing, 1972).

Marriage and Divorce (USA: Presbyterian and Reformed Publishing, 1980).

The Christian Counselor's Manual (USA: Presbyterian and Reformed Publishing, 1973).

Christian Living in the Home (USA: Presbyterian and Reformed Publishing, 1978).

Bannerman, J., *The Church of Christ, 2 vols.* (Cherry Hill, NJ: Mack Publishing Company, 1972).

Baxter, R., *The Reformed Pastor* (Edinburgh: The Banner of Truth Trust, 1979).

Berghoef, G and De Koster, L., *The Elders Handbook: A Practical Guide for Church Leaders* (Grand Rapids, MI: Christian's Library Press, 1979).

The Deacons Handbook: A Manual of Stewardship (Grand Rapids, MI: Christian's Library Press, 1980).

Hiscox, E. T., *Principles and Practices for Baptist Churches* (Grand Rapids, MI.: Kergel Publications, 1982).

Hulse, Erroll, *The Free Offer of the Gospel* (booklet) (Carey Publications Ltd, 1973).

'What is a Pastor?', *Reformation Today*, No. 249, 2012 (Sept–Oct), pp. 9–16.

Jefferson, C., *The Minister as Shepherd* (Virginia: Scripture Truth Book Co., n.d.).

Keddie, J. W., *The Church: Its Nature, Ordinance and Offices* (Scottish Reformed Heritage Pub., 2018).

Knox, D. B., *Sent by Jesus* (Edinburgh: The Banner of Truth Trust, 1992)

Lane, E. *Special Children: A Theology of Childhood* (Grace Publications, 1966).

Lloyd-Jones, D. M., *Preaching and Preachers* (London: Hodder & Stoughton, 1971).

Spiritual Depression: its Causes & Cures (London: Pickering & Inglis Ltd, 1965).

Murray, I. H., *The Reformation of the Church* (Edinburgh: The Banner of Truth Trust, 1987).

Murray, J., *Divorce* (USA: Presbyterian and Reformed Publishing, 1975).

Olyott, S., *Ministering like the Master* (Edinburgh: The Banner of Truth Trust, 2003).

Packer, J. I., *A Quest for Godliness* (Wheaton, Ill.: Crossway Books, 1990).

Pederson, R. J., *The Puritans: Daily Readings* (Fearn: Christian Heritage Imprint, 2012).

Piper, J., & Carson, D. A., *The Pastor as Scholar & the Scholar as Pastor* (Nottingham: IVP, 2011).

Pond, C., *Only Servants* (London: Grace Publications, 1991).

Read, D. R., *Growing Through Grief* (Croydon: FIEC, no date—booklet).

Shedd, W. G. T., *Homiletics & Pastoral Theology* (London: Banner of Truth Trust, 1969).

Spurgeon, C. H., *Lectures to my Students* (Edinburgh: Marshall, Morgan and Scott, 1958).

Still, W., *The Work of the Pastor* (Fern: Christian Focus, 2001).

Taylor, J., *Pastors under pressure* (Leominster, Day One Publishers, 2001).

Webb, R. A., *The Reformed Doctrine of Adoption* (Grand Rapids, MI: Eerdmans Publishing, 1947).

Wray, D. E., *Biblical Church Discipline* (Edinburgh: Banner of Truth Trust, 1978).

White, R. E. O., *A Guide to Pastoral Care* (London: Pickering and Inglis, 1976).

Appendix 7: Book list

Books by Rev Ian S McNaughton (published by Day One—formerly LDOS).

- *Opening Up Colossians and Philemon*, a short commentary (2006).

- *Opening Up 2 Thessalonians*, a short commentary (2008).

- *Darwin and Darwinism: Bible faith and the Christian worldview*, co-written (2009).

- *The* Real *Lord's Prayer: Christ's glory and grace in John 17* (2012).

- *Opening Up Job*, a short commentary (2014).

- *Getting to grips with Prayer: its realities, challenges and potential* (2017).

- *Engaging with Islam: an evangelical doctrinal perspective* (2019).

- *Opening Up 1 John*, a short commentary (2020).

- *The Resurrection: its message and meaning* (2021).

- *He Died, Was Buried, Is Risen* (A6 booklet, 2022).

- *Down from His glory: the Christmas reality* (A6 booklet, 2022).